Health Services Management

A BOOK OF CASES
Fifth Edition

Health Services Management

A BOOK OF CASES
Fifth Edition

Edited by
Anthony R. Kovner and
Duncan Neuhauser

AUPHA Press

Health Administration Press
Chicago, Illinois

7-14-99

Copyright © 1997 by the Foundation of the American College of Healthcare Executives. Printed in the United States of America. All rights reserved. This book or parts thereof may not be reproduced in any form without written permission of the publisher. Opinions and views expressed in this book are those of the author and do not necessarily reflect those of the Foundation of the American College of Healthcare Executives or the Association of University Programs in Health Administration.

01   00   99   5   4   3

Library of Congress Cataloging-in-Publication Data

Health services management : a book of cases / edited by Anthony R. Kovner and Duncan Neuhauser. — 5th ed.
    p.   cm.
Includes bibliographical references and index.
ISBN 1-56793-059-X (softbound : alk. paper)
    1. Health facilities—Administration—Case studies.   2. Health services administration—Case studies.   3. Hospitals—Administration—Case studies.
RA971.H43   1997 Suppl.
362.1'068—dc21   97-16063
                                       CIP

The paper used in this publication meets the minimum requirements of American National Standard for Information Sciences—Permanence of Paper for Printed Library Materials, ANSI Z39.48-1984. ∞™

Health Administration Press
A division of the Foundation
  of the American College of
  Healthcare Executives
One North Franklin Street
Suite 1700
Chicago, Illinois, 60606
(312) 424-2800

Association of University Programs
  in Health Administration
1911 North Fort Myer Drive, Suite 503
Arlington, VA 22209
(703) 524-5500

Contents

v

Preface to the Fifth Edition

This book was developed as a complementary text to our book, *Health Services Management: Readings and Commentary*, first published in 1978, sixth edition in 1997. We are delighted, in response to user demand and a need to keep more of the cases current, to prepare this fifth edition of our casebook.

We use the same organizing framework as in the book of readings: the health manager, control, organization design, clinician integration, adaptation, and accountability. The casebook can stand on its own, however, in teaching students and managers through the case method approach.

The fifth edition contains fourteen cases, seven of which are new or updated and seven of which have been retained as is from the fourth edition. Several of the cases can be used to illustrate more than one aspect of our organizing framework. In addition, we have added eleven one-page cases, all of which are new for this edition.

All of these cases have been tested in the classroom. They have been selected because they take place in a variety of settings from the perspective of managers who must define and respond to particular complex situations.

Anthony R. Kovner
Duncan Neuhauser
1997

Learning Through the Case Method

Anthony R. Kovner

A challenge for many graduate programs in health services management is bridging the gap between theory and skills and their application by students to health services organizations. Part of the problem lies in the difficulty of attracting and retaining skilled teachers who can integrate perspectives and apply concepts across disciplines in responding to managerial problems and opportunities.

A second challenge is to prepare graduates to communicate effectively, in writing and orally, and to assist them in working effectively in groups. This includes helping students to assess the effects of their personalities or behavioral styles on others. Is the student perceived as abrasive, wishywashy, manipulative? Is the student aware of how others interpret not only his words but his tone and body language?

Students in graduate programs of health services management need to understand their own values and those of others who differ in educational background, political and religious orientation, clinical experience, or the careers and orientations of parents and siblings.

A "case" is a description of a situation or problem that is actually faced by a manager and that requires analysis, decision, and planning of a course of action. A decision may be to delay a decision, and a planned course of action may be to take no action. A case takes place in time. A case must have an issue. As McNair says: "There must be a question of what should somebody do, what should somebody have done, who is to blame for the situation, what is the best decision to be made under the circumstances."[1] A case represents selection from a situation; it represents selection by the casewriter.

Case method involves class discussion, guided by a teacher so that students can diagnose and define important problems in a situation, acquire competence in developing useful alternatives to respond to such problems, and improve judgment in selecting action alternatives. Students learn ways both to diagnose constraints and opportunities faced by the manager in implementation and to overcome constraints, given limited time and dollars.

Teachers can transmit great quantities of data to students more effectively and certainly more efficiently by lecture. The teacher is assumed to be correct in presenting facts, and the student transcribes key points of the lecture and transmits them back to the teacher at examination time.

In a case course, the teacher's job is to engage the students in a management simulation so that they can think independently, communicate effectively, and defend their opinions logically with reference to underlying assumptions and values. Often a case has no one right answer because, in dealing with issues, there are at least two sides to a question.

It is often difficult for students to adjust to a classroom in which there is no authority figure, no lectures from which to take notes, and little information offered by the teacher, at least until the class discussion has ended. Some students find it irritating to have to listen to their peers when they are paying to learn what the teacher has to say.

In a case course, students learn how to use information at the point of decision. Many students dislike "putting themselves on the line" when they are "only" students saying what they think. If there are no "right" answers, students quickly learn in a case course that there are many "wrong" answers in terms of faulty logic or assumptions challenged or contradicted by their peers. Students fear looking foolish and being downgraded accordingly by the teacher. And they must pass the course.[2] But students should consider such self-exposure to be little enough cost to pay in relation to the benefit of appearing mature and skillful after graduation and in the professional environment. It is hoped that they will have gained judgment and will have learned how to behave and communicate their opinions to others.

As Cantor[3] says, "You don't learn from anybody else's experience or from your own experience unless you go through the experience to learn." This is what the case method has to offer students—an experience in learning that involves testing opinions and conclusions against the reality of the case and the judgment of peers and teacher.

How do cases bridge the gap between theory and skills and their application by managers? Problems that health services managers face do not come neatly packaged as separate questions of statistics, economics, organization theory, or policy analysis. Rather they are organizational, multidisciplinary problems, sometimes difficult to define as well as to resolve. Problems may include negotiating a new contract with the chief of radiology, responding appropriately to patient complaints, or taking responsibility for quality assurance in relation to a surgeon's poor performance.

Student performance in a case course is typically assessed on participation in class and on written analysis of case materials. A lack of sufficient time by the teacher in analyzing a student's evaluation may be partially corrected by allowing peer evaluation as well. Often teachers ask students to collaborate on complex cases or to evaluate each other's performance. The presenting student should be told if personal style or mannerisms interfere with a case analysis presentation or with its perception by others.

In a case course, students are often asked to adopt the perspectives of certain characters in the case, to play certain roles. To deny someone of something or to persuade someone to do something requires an understanding of that person's needs and perceptions of the decision maker. Role-playing can promote a better understanding of viewpoints that otherwise may seem irrational given a student's prior understanding of what should be done in a particular situation. Students can better understand their own values and underlying assumptions when their opinions are challenged by peers and teachers.

To conclude, it is important to understand what a case is not and what case method cannot teach. Cases are not real life—they present only part of a situation. Writing or communicating a case may be as difficult or more difficult than evaluating someone else's written case. Like many a consultant, the student can never see the results—what would have happened if the case participants had followed his advice.

There are some aspects of management that can only be learned by managing. How else to understand when someone says one thing but means another? How else to judge when, if ever, to confront or oppose a member of the ruling coalition when that member's behavior appears to threaten the long-range interests of the organization? Students and managers have to form and adopt their own value systems and make their own decisions. A case course can give students a better understanding of the nature of the role they will be playing as managers—an understanding that can help them to manage better, if not well.

Notes

1. Andrew R. Towl, *To Study Administration by Cases* (Boston: Graduate School of Business Administration, Harvard University, 1969), p. 67.
2. Ibid., p. 68.
3. Ibid., p. 155.

A Short History of the Case Method of Teaching

Karen Schachter Weingrod
Duncan Neuhauser

Teaching by example is no doubt as old as the first parent and child. In medicine it surely started with a healer, the first apprentice, and a patient. The ancient Greeks codified medical principles, rules, and laws. University education in medicine started about 800 years ago, focused on abstract principles and scholastic reasoning, and was removed from practicality. By 1750 in England, the professions aspired to gentlemen status.[1] The goldheaded cane of the English physician, for instance, was the clear symbol that his hands were not expected to touch patients, unlike the hands of apothecaries and barber surgeons. Later, the American sociologist Thorstein Veblen, in *The Theory of the Leisure Class*, used the example of the cane as symbolic that a gentleman need not work with his hands.[2] In the late 1700s in France, medical education moved into hospitals or "the clinic," where patients in large numbers could be observed, autopsies performed, and the physiological state linked back to the patients' signs and symptoms.[3] This was one step in the departure from the abstract medical theorizing in universities (often about the "four humours"), which may have had no bearing on actual disease processes.

Education in law also became increasingly abstract, conveyed through the erudite lecture. It built theoretical constructs and was logically well reasoned. The professor spoke and the student memorized and recited without much opportunity for practical experience or discussion. This had become the standard by the late 1850s.

It is only by comparison with what went on before in universities that the case method of teaching represented such a striking change. The historical development of the case method can be traced to Harvard University. Perhaps it is not surprising that this change occurred in the United States rather than in Europe, with the American inclinations toward democratic equality, practicality, and positivism, and the lack of interest in classic abstract theorizing.

The change started in 1870 when the president of Harvard University, Charles William Eliot, appointed the obscure lawyer Christopher Columbus Langdell to be dean of the Harvard Law School.

Langdell believed law to be a science. In his own words: "Law considered as a science, consists of certain principles or doctrines. To have such a mastery of these as to be able to apply them with constant faculty and certainty to the ever-tangled skein of human affairs, is what constitutes a good lawyer; and hence to acquire that mastery should be the business of every earnest student of the law."[4]

The specimens needed for the study of Langdell's science of law were judicial opinions as recorded in books and stored in libraries. He accepted the science of law, but he turned the learning process back to front. Instead of giving a lecture that would define a principle of law and give supporting examples of judicial opinions, he gave the students the judicial opinions without the principle and by use of a Socratic dialogue extracted from the students in the classroom the principles that would make sense out of the cases. The student role was now active rather than passive. Students were subjected to rigorous questioning of the case material. They were asked to defend their judgments and to confess to error when their judgments were illogical. Although this dialectic was carried on by the professor and one or two students at a time, all of the students learned and were on the edge of their seats, fearing or hoping to be called on next. The law school style that evolved has put the student under public pressure to reason quickly, clearly, and coherently in a way that is valuable in the courtroom or during negotiation. After a discouraging start Langdell attracted such able instructors as Oliver Wendell Holmes, Jr. They carried the day, and now the case method of teaching is nearly universal in American law schools.

The introduction of the case method of teaching to medicine is also known. A Harvard medical student of the class of 1901, Walter B. Cannon shared a room with Harry Bigelow, a third-year law student. The excitement with which Bigelow and his classmates debated the issues within the cases they were reading for class contrasted sharply with the passivity of medical school lectures.

In 1900, discussing the value of the case method in medicine, Harvard President Charles Eliot described the earlier medical education as follows:

> I think it was thirty-five years ago that I was a lecturer at the Harvard Medical School for one winter; at that time lectures began in the school at eight o'clock in the morning and went on steadily till two o'clock—six mortal hours, one

after the other of lectures, without a question from the professor, without the possibility of an observation by the student, none whatever, just the lecture to be listened to, and possibly taken notes of. Some of the students could hardly write.[5]

In December 1899, Cannon persuaded one of his instructors, G. L. Walton, to present one of the cases in written form from his private practice as an experiment. Walton printed a sheet with the patient's history and allowed the students a week to study it. The lively discussion that ensued in class made Walton an immediate convert.[6] Other faculty soon followed, including Richard C. Cabot.

Through the case method, medical students would learn to judge and interpret clinical data, to estimate the value of evidence, and to recognize the gaps in their knowledge—something that straight lecturing could never reveal. The case method of teaching allowed students to throw off passivity in the lecture hall and integrate their knowledge of anatomy, physiology, pathology, and therapeutics into a unified mode of thought.

As a student Cannon wrote two articles about the case method in 1900 for the *Boston Medical and Surgical Journal* (later to become *The New England Journal of Medicine*).[7] He sent a copy of one of these papers to the famous clinician professor Dr. William Osler of Johns Hopkins University. Osler replied, "I have long held that the only possible way of teaching students the subject of medicine is by personal daily contact with cases, which they study not only once or twice, but follow systematically."[8] If a written medical case was interesting, a real live patient in the classroom could be memorable. Osler regularly introduced patients to his class, asked students to interview and examine the patient and discuss the medical problems involved. He would regularly send students to the library and laboratory to seek answers and report back to the rest of the class.[9] This is ideal teaching. Osler's students worshipped him, but with today's division of labor in medicine between basic science and clinical medicine, such a synthesis is close to impossible.

The May 24, 1900 issue of the *Boston Medical and Surgical Journal* was devoted to articles and comments by Eliot, Cannon, Cabot, and others about the case method of teaching. In some ways this journal issue remains the best general discussion of the case method. This approach was adopted rapidly at other medical schools, and books of written cases quickly followed in neurology (1902), surgery (1904), and orthopedic surgery (1905).[10]

Walter Cannon went on to a distinguished career in medical research. Richard C. Cabot joined the medical staff of the Massachusetts General Hospital, and in 1906 published his first book of cases. (He also introduced the first social worker into a hospital.)[11] He was concerned about the undesirable separation of clinical physicians and pathologists; too many diagnoses were xviii   Short History of the Case Method

turning out to be false at autopsy. To remedy this, Cabot began to hold his case exercises with students, house officers, and visitors.

Cabot's clinical/pathological conferences took on a stereotypical style and eventually were adopted in teaching hospitals throughout the world. First, the patient's history, symptoms, and test results would be described. Then an invited specialist would discuss the case, suggest an explanation, and give a diagnosis. Finally, the pathologist would present the autopsy or pathological diagnosis and questions would follow to elaborate points.

In 1915, Cabot sent written copies of his cases to interested physicians as "at home case method exercises." These became so popular that in 1923 the *Boston Medical and Surgical Journal* began to publish one per issue.[12] This journal has since changed its name to *The New England Journal of Medicine*, but the "Cabot Case Records" still appear with each issue.

A look at a current *New England Journal of Medicine* case will show how much the case method has changed since Christopher Columbus Langdell's original concept. The student or house officer is no longer asked to discuss the case; rather, it is the expert who puts her reputation on the line. She has the opportunity to demonstrate wisdom, but can also be refuted in front of a large audience. Although every physician in the audience probably makes mental diagnoses, the case presentation has become a passive affair, like a lecture.

Richard Cabot left the Massachusetts General Hospital to head the Social Relations (sociology, psychology, cultural anthropology) Department at Harvard. He brought the case method with him, but it disappeared from use there by the time of his death in 1939.[13] The social science disciplines were concerned with theory building, hypothesis testing, and research methodology, and to such "unapplied" pure scientists perhaps the case method was considered primitive. Further, the use of the case method of teaching also diminished in the first two preclinical years of medical school as clinical scientists came more and more to the fore with their laboratory work and research on physiology, pharmacology, biochemistry, and molecular biology. Currently a return to a problem-solving focus in medical school is being advocated by a task force of the American Association of Medical Colleges.

In 1908, the Harvard Business School was created as a department of the Graduate School of Arts and Sciences. It was initially criticized as merely a school for "successful money-making." Early on an effort was made to teach through the use of written problems involving situations faced by actual business executives, presented in sufficient factual detail to enable students to develop their own decisions. The school's first book of cases, on marketing, was published in 1922 by Melvin T. Copeland.[14]

Today, nearly every class in the Harvard Business School is taught by the case method. In 1957, the Intercollegiate Case Clearing House was founded.

Physically located on the Harvard campus, it housed approximately 40,000 cases and added 1,000 to 1,200 new cases each year. Cases were made available to other universities. Recently the clearing house was renamed HBS Case Services and now limits itself to cases produced at the Harvard Business School.

Unlike the law school, where cases come directly from judicial decisions (sometimes abbreviated by the instructor) and the medical school, where the patient is the basis for the case, the business faculty and their aides must enter organizations to collect and compile their material. This latter mode of selection offers substantial editorial latitude. Here more than elsewhere the case writer's vision, or lack of it, defines the content of the case.

Unlike a pathologist's autopsy diagnosis, a business case is not designed to have a right answer. In fact, one usually never knows whether the business in question lives or dies. Rather, the cases are written in a way that splits a large class (up to 80 students) into factions. The best cases are those that create divergent opinions; the professor becomes more an orchestra leader than a source of truth. The professor's opinion or answer may never be made explicit. Following a discussion, a student's question related to what really happened or what should have been done may be answered, "I don't know" or "I think the key issues were picked up in the case discussion." Such hesitancy on the part of the instructor is often desirable. To praise or condemn a particular faction in the classroom can discourage future discussions.

The class atmosphere in a business school is likely to be less pressured than in a law school. Like a good surgeon, a good lawyer must often think very quickly, but unlike the surgeon his thinking is demonstrated verbally and publicly. He must persuade by the power of his logic rather than by force of authority. Business and management are different. Key managerial decisions— "What business are we in?" "Who are our customers?" "Where should we be ten years from now?"—may take months or even years to answer.

The fact that the business manager's time frame reduces the pressure for immediate answers makes management education different from physician education in other ways. Physicians are required to absorb countless facts on anatomy, disease symptoms, and drug side effects. Confronted with 20 patients a day, the physician has no time to consult references and must rely on memory instead. The manager can look up information, given the longer time horizon of decision making in business. Therefore, managerial education focuses more on problem-solving techniques than on memorization of data.

Not all business schools have endorsed the case method of teaching. The University of Chicago Business School, for example, rarely uses cases and focuses on teaching the "science" of economics, human behavior, and operations research. The faculty are concerned with theory building, hypothesis testing, statistical methodology, and the social sciences. Stanford Business

School uses about half social sciences and half case method. Each school is convinced that its teaching philosophy is best and believes others to be misguided. Conceptually, the debate can be broken into two aspects: science versus professionalism, and active versus passive learning.

There is little question that active student involvement in learning is better than a passive listening to lectures. The case method is one of many approaches to increasing student participation. However, only a skilled instructor, for example, can stimulate a lively discussion by social sciences students on the theoretical assumptions, methodological problems, and use or abuse of statistical analysis in an *American Journal of Sociology* assignment.

Academic science is not overly concerned with the practical problems of the world, but professionals are and professional education should be. The lawyer, physician, and manager cannot wait for perfect knowledge; they have to make decisions "in the face of uncertainty." Science can help with these decisions to varying degrees. To the extent that scientific theories have the power to predict and explain, they can be used by professionals. In the jargon of statistics: the higher the percentage of variance explained, the more useful the scientific theory, the smaller the role for clinical or professional judgment, and the greater the role for case method teaching as opposed to, for example, mathematical problem-solving.

It can be argued that the professional will always be working at the frontier of the limits of scientific prediction. When science is the perfect predictor, then often the problem is solved, or the application is delegated to computers or technicians, or, as in some branches of engineering, professional skills focus on the manipulation of accurate but complex mathematical equations.

Scientific medicine now understands smallpox so well that it no longer exists. Physicians spend most of their time on problems that are not solved: cancer, heart disease, or the common complaints of living that bring most people to doctors. In management, the budget cycle, personnel position control, sterile operating room environment, and maintenance of the business office ledgers are handled routinely by organizational members and usually do not consume the attention of the chief executive officer. In law, the known formulations become the "boiler plate" of contracts.

The debate between business schools over the use of cases illustrates the difference in belief in the power of the social sciences in the business environment. Teaching modes related to science and judgment will always be in uneasy balance with each other, shifting with time and place. A few innovative medical schools have moved away from the scientific lectures of the preclinical years and toward a case problem–solving mode (e.g., the University of Limburg in Maastricht, Holland). On the other side of the coin, a quiet revolution is being waged in clinical reasoning. The principles of statistics, epidemiology, and economics, filtered through the techniques of decision analysis, cost-effectiveness analysis, computer modeling, and artificial intelligence, are making the Cabot Case Record approach obsolete for clinical reasoning. Scientific methods of clinical reasoning are beginning to replace aspects of professional or clinical judgment in medicine.[15]

This does not mean that the professional aspect of medicine will be eliminated by computer-based science. Rather, the frontiers, the unknown areas calling for professional judgment, will shift to new areas, such as the development of socio-emotional rapport with patients—what used to be called "the bedside manner."

The cases that make up this book are derived from the business school style of case teaching. As such they do not have answers. The cases can be used to apply management concepts to practical problems; however, these concepts (scientific theory seems too strong a term to apply to them) may help solve these case problems but will not yield the "one right answer." They all leave much room for debate.

Notes

1. Harold J. Cook, *The Decline of the Old Medical Regime in Stuart London* (Ithaca, NY: Cornell University Press, 1986).
2. Thorstein Veblen, *The Theory of the Leisure Class* (1899; reprinted New York: Mentor, 1953).
3. Michel Foucault, *The Birth of the Clinic* (New York: Vintage, 1973).
4. C. C. Langdell, *Cases and Contracts* (1871), cited in *The Law at Harvard*, by Arthur E. Sutherland (Cambridge, MA: Harvard University Press, 1967), p. 174.
5. Charles Eliot, "The Inductive Method Applied to Medicine," *Boston Medical and Surgical Journal* 142, no. 22 (24 May 1900): 557.
6. Saul Benison, A. Clifford Barger, and Elin L. Wolfe, *Walter B. Cannon, The Life and Times of a Young Scientist* (Cambridge, MA: Harvard University Press, 1987), pp. 65–75, 417–418.
7. W. B. Cannon, "The Case Method of Teaching Systematic Medicare," *Boston Medical and Surgical Journal* 142, no. 2 (11 January 1900): 31–36; and "The Case System in Medicine," 142, no. 22 (24 May 1900): 563–64.
8. Benison et al., *Walter B. Cannon . . .* p. 66.
9. Alan M. Chesney, *The Johns Hopkins Hospital and the Johns Hopkins University School of Medicine*, Vol. 11, 1893–1905 (Baltimore, MD: The Johns Hopkins Press, 1958), pp. 125–28.
10. Benison et al., *Walter B. Cannon . . .* p. 418.
11. Although not the first hospital-based social worker to work with Cabot, his best known social worker colleague was Walter Cannon's sister, Ida Cannon. Ibid., p. 145.
12. These cases start October 25, 1923.

13. Paul Buck (ed.), *The Social Sciences at Harvard* (Boston, MA: Harvard University Press, 1965).
14. For more on the history of the case method of teaching managers see Roy Penchansky, *Health Services Administration: Policy Cases and the Case Method* (Boston, MA: Harvard University Press, 1968), pp. 395–453.
15. The proposal to increase the problem-solving content of medical education is found in Association of American Medical Colleges, *Graduate Medical Education: Proposals for the Eighties* (Washington, DC: AAMC, 1980). Also reprinted as a supplement in *Journal of Medical Education* 56, no. 9 (September 1981, part 2).

Part I

The Role of the Manager

Introduction

Personnel decisions, critical to managerial effectiveness, are often postponed by managers. Considerably more time may be spent on the decision to purchase or lease a piece of equipment costing $800,000 with a useful life of seven years than on the decision to hire a registered nurse earning $40,000 who may work for the organization for twenty years. Because there are so few managers compared to other employees and staff, health services executives often are more careful in selecting their own subordinates or colleagues.

An important aspect of employing a manager is determining the time to spend on the search and the amount of funds to expend on advertising. Someone must decide who will screen candidates, who will check references, how many candidates to interview, and who should see the job applicant.

Perhaps even more important than the hiring decision is the continuous evaluation and motivation of subordinates and colleagues, many of whom may have been hired by the manager's predecessors. If a manager is not performing at the level of competence her supervisor expects, what are the latter's options? What are the manager's options if she disagrees with her supervisor's expectations or evaluation? If the supervising manager does not fire or transfer the manager being evaluated, her own effectiveness may suffer because she lacks a key aide to implement her decisions or augment her politically. But this ineffective manager may have been working loyally in the organization for many years, and there are costs involved in searching for and training a new manager as well as the risk that a new hire's behavior will not be as anticipated.

Managerial personnel decisions become even more complicated when the health services manager, as in "the Associate Director and the Controllers," is dealing with a functional specialist who is line-responsible to the top manager and staff-responsible to the chief controller in a multi-unit medical center. The straight and dotted lines of authority on the organizational chart become fuzzy and difficult to agree on, especially when the associate director's boss and the boss medical center director of finance distrust each other. In this selection, key staff of two recently merged units have different value orientations—the base hospital primarily serving attending physicians in their private practice and the ambulatory health services program emphasizing the provision of respectful patient care to the needy.

Management is often a lonely occupation and preoccupation. Important decisions are seldom made on an either-or basis and usually involve personal as well as organizational benefits and risks. In "A New Faculty Practice Administrator for the Department of Medicine," the weighing of risks and benefits is different for Sam Bones, the chief of medicine, than it is for Sandra Compson, the group practice administrator, or for Compson's eventual successor. Similarly, in "The Associate Director and the Controllers," the stakes of the game are higher for Jim Joel, the ambulatory health services program administrator, and for Percy Oram, its controller, than for Milton Schlitz, the medical center director of finance, and for Miller Harrang, the chief executive officer of the ambulatory health services program.

Why must Joel decide to do anything at all? In "A New Faculty Practice Administrator," Bones must choose a new group practice administrator. But in "The Associate Director and the Controllers," Joel can decide not to get involved and allow Harrang and Schlitz to deal with the consequences of Oram's ineffectiveness. How much should it matter to Joel whether Oram remains in the job or not, so long as Joel can protect his own job? On the other hand, Joel is being paid to manage, not to observe nor to protect himself. Good management generally makes a difference to the paying customer and, more importantly for the manager, to the ruling coalition of the organization. How much of a difference it makes is open to debate. But no one will look after the manager's interest if he will not look after it himself. This is a first rule of managerial self-preservation and of managerial system maintenance. Looking after oneself does not mean that the manager should lock the office door and read reports. Nor does it require offending those in the ruling coalition perceived to be acting against the long-term organizational interest. In a rare case, there may be benefits for the manager in offending members of the ruling coalition. The costs of not offending them may also be great. But the manager should first weigh whether he is willing to pay the consequences of offending such members, in terms of his own authority and position.

Health services managers often face tremendous pressures from the government to move in a certain direction, and resistance from physicians, who are urging not one iota of movement further than that required by the letter of the law. If a strategic plan developed by consultants assumes increases of 20 percent in unduplicated patient count in the service area, the manager may be persuaded (or may persuade herself) to accept the assumption to assure board approval, although a 5 percent increase is more likely. The manager can always defend her decision, and the deficiency in her estimates may seem less important after the plan is accepted and new marketing staff has been hired.

Perhaps not. Pfeffer and Salancik have argued that the contribution of managers accounts for about 10 percent of the variance in organizational performance, and that "the sportscasters' cliche that managers are hired to be fired reflects a great amount of truth about all managers."[1] There is a great amount of evidence, however, that managers *do* make a difference in organizational performance, that is, if only because managers often play a principal role in obtaining resources for the organization, to which function Pfeffer and Salancik place such high priority. In any event, the contribution of health services managers to organizational effectiveness is being perceived as increasingly important, and managerial rewards and risks have been increasing.

If the health services manager can never meet all the expectations of key participants in her organization, she can at least be perceived by them as taking their interests into account in policy formulation and implementation. Unfortunately, this involves regular communication with numerous participants, the time for which is not always available—although, perhaps, more available than most managers are willing to admit. We are assuming that key participants prefer to trust the manager (rather than get rid of her) based on her stated willingness to implement specified and agreed-upon organizational goals with which they may not personally agree.

What makes for an effective manager? The answer depends on who answers as well as on a given manager's actual actions or actions perceived by superiors, subordinates, and peers. Sometimes an effective manager—as in the case of "The Nowhere Job"—should consider resigning. Clearly, the health services manager must acquire certain information, must possess certain skills, and must have certain values consistent with the organizational context in which she functions. It is not always easy to decide what to do after the manager receives disquieting information such as that shown in the case of "Manager Morale of Uptown Hospital."

In assessing the four applicants for the position of group practice administrator or in evaluating Associate Director Joel's performance in the two cases in this section, ask yourself the following questions:

1. Do these managers have adequate knowledge of the power structure of their organizations and institutional environments, and an understanding of key participants who can affect their activities and responsibilities?

2. Do they possess the necessary interpersonal and analytical skills to function effectively?

3. Have they shown good judgment in making or in not making certain decisions?

4. Do they have personalities appropriate to their job situations and to the people with whom they are working?

Evaluating managerial effectiveness or contribution carries a cost. All pertinent information may not be available. Reliance on measuring managerial performance may divert attention inappropriately from the manager's overall performance to criteria that can be measured easily.

Ensuring financial flows to the health services organization is an important criterion for effective managerial performance. And yet, despite the importance of financial flows, there is considerable ambiguity about this criterion in Bones's faculty group practice, relative to the research and teaching goals of the department of medicine, and in Joel's health center, relative to providing free and respectful patient care to the indigent and sick. For there may be considerable feeling among the staff involved that the financial flows will continue, regardless of the success of the group practice in attracting more patients or of whether the health center is succeeding in collecting more dollars from the indigent.

Evaluating managers, like management itself, involves judgment, which in Ray Brown's phrase, is "knowledge ripened by experience."[2] We are hopeful that these cases can be useful in ripening student judgment, in clarifying for students the assumptions on which they will make future decisions.

Case Questions

A New Faculty Practice Administrator for the Department of Medicine

- What criteria would you use in evaluating the four candidates?
- What are the strengths and weaknesses of each candidate?
- What are Bones's criteria in evaluating the four candidates?
- Whom would you recommend to Bones as your selection for the position? Why?

The Associate Director and the Controllers

- What is the problem from Joel's point of view? From Oram's point of view? From Harrang's and Schlitz's points of view?
- In what ways should Oram be accountable to Joel and Schlitz?
- Given that Oram's performance is not acceptable to Joel, what options does Joel have to affect Oram's performance?

- What do you recommend that Joel do now? Why?
- What are the constraints on effective implementation of your recommendations, and how might Joel overcome them?
- What should Joel have done differently prior to the end point of the case that might have made the problem easier to solve now?
- What conflict is there between the goals of Joel and Schlitz? In the face of such conflict what are Oram's options in responding, and what would you recommend that Oram do now and why?

Notes

1. Jeffrey Pfeffer and Gerald R. Salancik, *The External Control of Organizations* (New York: Harper and Row, 1978), p. 17.
2. Ray Brown, *Judgment in Administration* (New York: McGraw-Hill, 1966), p. 9.

Selected Bibliography

Brown, Lawrence D. *Politics and Health Care Organization*. Washington, DC: The Brookings Institution, 1983, pp. 75–129.

Griffith, John R. *The Well-Managed Community Hospital*, 3rd Edition. Chicago: Health Administration Press, 1995, pp. 135–176.

Kovner, Anthony R., and Alan H. Channing. *Really Trying: A Career Guide for the Health Services Manager*, 2nd Edition. Chicago: Health Administration Press, 1994.

Leebov, W., and G. Scott. *Health Care Managers in Transition: Shifting Roles and Changing Organizations*. San Francisco: Jossey-Bass, 1990.

Ross, Austin. *Cornerstones of Leadership for Health Services Executives*. Chicago: Health Administration Press, 1992.

Zuckerman, Howard S., and William C. Dowling. "The Managerial Role." *Essentials of Health Care Management*, Albany, NY: Delmar, 1997, pp. 30–54.

Case 1

A New Faculty Practice Administrator for the Department of Medicine

Anthony R. Kovner

Sandra Compson was leaving her position as faculty practice administrator at Wise Medical Center to raise a family. Dr. Sam Bones, chief of medicine, asked Compson before leaving to become involved in the selection of her replacement.

The faculty practice in the department of medicine was formally launched three years ago in 1990, as were faculty practices in other medical departments.

Wise Medical Center is regarded as one of the largest and best-managed hospitals in Eastern City. The CEO, Dr. Worthy, was appointed in 1978. He has captained the dramatic growth of the medical center, its financial success, and the improvement of its medical teaching programs. Over the last five years, almost all the clinical chiefs have been replaced. Internal medicine is the largest department in the medical center. Dr. Bones is a specialist in cardiovascular disease, and has an excellent reputation as a clinician.

His department has grown very large, and Bones has difficulty in staffing the large number of beds with medical residents. Bones is praised for his leadership skills, his intelligence, and his caring for those who work with him. He has been criticized for his unwillingness to make tough decisions regarding the economics of the department and for not getting rid of physicians who don't or won't meet his own and departmental high standards of quality. The medical center and the department face stiff financial pressures, and Dr. Worthy and others are trying to determine what the medical center's response to managed care should be. The medical center currently only has referral arrangements with several large health maintenance organizations (HMO).

There are 13 medical sub-specialties and approximately 45 physicians who use the faculty practice suite. The faculty practice staff includes the following: two receptionists, one secretary, three medical technicians, and one administrator. Larger physician practices bring secretarial support when the physicians are seeing patients in the suite. (These include infectious disease, urology and radiation oncology).

Ambulatory care facilities of the group include ten examining rooms, appropriate supporting areas for reception and waiting, a small laboratory, a technician's area, a billing office, and an office for the administrator. The space is often overcrowded, yet sometimes underutilized. Most physicians have block-time appointments and Compson has estimated that they use only 50 percent of the block time to actually see patients, while other physicians complain that they cannot get Faculty Practice Plan (FPP) suite time to see their patients.

Compson is not privy to the revenue figures for the faculty practice as billing is done separately by the hospital's finance department.

The FPP suite is open 9 a.m. to 5 p.m. Monday through Friday. Visits have increased from 1,500 per month in 1990 to 3,000 per month in 1992. Demand is such that if more staff and space were available, another 1,500 visits per month might be carried out with little or no targeted marketing.

The computerized billing system is not kept in the suite but a terminal access is available. The physicians' offices have no knowledge of group finances. Registration and scheduling are not computerized. There is no room in the suite for chart storage. The physicians' offices must schedule their own patient appointments. Physicians are seeing two patients an hour when in proper facilities they could be seeing three. Physicians do not have their own rooms but rotate according to room availability.

The original operating concept of the faculty practice suite was as a place with an upscale ambiance where physicians could see their patients. The purpose for creating the suite was to recover scattered examination space throughout the medical center and to take advantage of economies of shared space. Based on these concepts, decisions were made early to maximize treatment space at the expense of chart storage space.

An HMO recently approached Compson seeking pediatric ambulatory care and guaranteeing 200 visits per month. But no space was available to accommodate this demand, which Compson believes could have been negotiated as a profitable service.

Bones's last interview with Compson went as follows:

Bones: Sandra, as you know, you've done a splendid job here this past year and we'll be sorry to lose you. The situation of the departmental faculty practice as I see it is this. During the past few years the practice has been organized and it has grown dramatically. We seem to be having a lot of operating problems, such as space, poor support for the physicians, and antiquated billing and scheduling systems. The question now is, what kind of a job needs to be done by the group administrator and who should we look at? What do you think?

Compson: Well, Dr. Bones, as you know, I've enjoyed tremendously the opportunity to work with you and with the members of the department and I will be sorry to leave, although I am looking forward very much to raising a family. I think that the kind of person you need is not necessarily the type of person you needed three years ago. Then you needed someone who could "put out fires" and try to keep the place working. Now I think you need a systems person who can make the place run more effectively, at the same time keeping up the morale of the staff and working with the physicians.

Bones: I agree with you. I want someone personable and energetic, who isn't afraid of work, who can get along with the doctors and the hospital administration. I think the most important thing is getting our physicians the kind of support they need to run a first-class faculty practice. The systems aren't working down there. The department isn't making the kind of money that it should be making, and we should be making it much more pleasant for our physicians to practice here. [See Illustration 1.1 for Faculty Practice Suite Billings and Collections, and Illustration 1.2 for Faculty Practice Suite Quarterly Statistics.]

Compson: As you know, per your instructions, I've started the interviewing process and will send you all the good candidates. I have spoken to

Illustration 1.1   Faculty Practice Suite Billings and Collections, Calendar Year 1992

Month	Billings	Collections	Gross Collection Rate
January	$308,076	$147,784	47.97%
February	$245,703	$142,090	57.83%
March	$245,211	$144,944	59.11%
April	$200,008	$171,407	85.70%
May	$301,075	$164,658	54.69%
June	$220,726	$165,677	75.06%
July	$259,163	$170,374	65.74%
August	$288,244	$159,860	55.46%
September	$248,275	$178,932	72.07%
YTD total	$2,316,481	$1,445,726	62.42%

Illustration 1.2   Faculty Practice Suite Quarterly Statistics: Departmental
Key Indicators, July 1, 1992–September 30, 1992

Item	This Period 1991	This Period 1992	YTD 1991	YTD 1992
Percent Overall Utilization	64	72	64	72
# MDs Participation	44	50	44	50
Monthly Visits	5,280	6,528	15,840	19,584
Total Income	$320,121	$488,851	$960,363	$1,445,726
Net Income/Less Expenses	$13,755	($1,658)	$34,991	$4,568

several directors of programs of healthcare administration and to the hospital human resources department. There aren't a lot of good people available with systems and management experience in healthcare. I don't want someone who is strictly a systems person. The manager must be in touch with the needs, wants, requirements, and expectations of the customers. I see the customers of the faculty practice as both the physicians and the patients.

Bones: Sandy, I agree with you there. I know you'll excuse me, but I have to attend an important strategic planning meeting for the hospital. I still don't quite understand what they're going to do, but I wish they'd give more emphasis in the plan to building up the medical center's research capabilities.

Compson: All right. Then I'll be getting back to you soon. I will make appointments with Renee, your secretary, for all the promising candidates.

One month after Sandra Compson's interview with Bones, she has completed interviews with 11 candidates for the position. She has eliminated from consideration four graduates from health administration programs who lack appropriate work experience and three medical center employees in the finance department whom she feels would not relate well to the physicians in the group. Compson has made tape recordings of all her interviews with the remaining four promising candidates, and has had difficulty in choosing among them.

Compson's first interview was with Dave O'Brien, currently assistant director for patient accounts in finance at the medical center. The second interview was with Sal Sorrentino, a June graduate from the City University program in health policy and management, and assistant director of a neighborhood health center prior to entering the graduate program. The third interview was with Marcia Rabin, a classmate of Sorrentino's at City University and director of human resources at a 200-bed nursing home prior to entering the graduate program. Finally, there is Bonnie Goldsmith, who has just completed two years with the Department of Health and Human Services (DHHS) in

Washington, DC, after graduating with a Master in Health Administration (MHA) from City. Compson has decided to review the tapes with Dr. Tim Brass, director of the medical center's continuous quality improvement program, who also practices in the faculty practice suite, before forwarding her recommendations to Bones.

David O'Brien

Compson (to Brass): The first interview is with Dave O'Brien, age 25. He wears conservative glasses and dresses conservatively. When I spoke to Barbara Karen, Wise Medical Center senior vice president of finance, she said that Dave was energetic and conscientious, and that he got things done. She recommended Dave highly for the position. If there was any weakness, Karen said that Dave was a hard driver, which sometimes antagonized the people under him. Dave had no problems, it seems, in getting along with his boss but not a lot of experience, if any, in working with physicians. (Compson plays a tape of the interview.)

    Compson: Dave, can you tell me in a few words something about your background and experience?

    O'Brien: Sure, Ms. Compson. I went to Upstate College where I was a business major. Then I started working in the hospital finance department as a biller and last year was appointed as assistant director in patient accounts. I intend to get my graduate degree at City University, in their MHA program.

    Compson: Going at night?

    O'Brien: Well, I don't think there will be any problem. Others have done it here at the medical center, and I want to get out of finance and into management.

    Compson: Dave, what would you say has been your greatest accomplishment in patient accounts?

    O'Brien: Well, Ms. Compson, I would say that I've really improved the system for billing and collections, starting with getting the bills out on time, all the way through to collections, and in refining and improving the data system that indicates how well we are doing. Performance has improved since I've taken the job—in speed, in accuracy, in the percentage collected, and in the time it takes for the hospital to get our money.

    Compson: Dave, that does sound impressive. If you were faculty practice administrator, what would you consider your greatest asset?

    O'Brien: I would say it's my ability to get a job done. There are too many people in this field who are just willing to go along with the way things have always been done until there's pressure from some quarter, and then it's often too late to do something, or too late to do it the right way.

Compson: And what would you say is your greatest liability?

O'Brien: Well, you know, in every organization some people are against change, because either it affects their own interest or because they just don't like change. After all, every change in somebody's department has to affect everyone involved in a relative if not in an absolute way. As my old teacher used to say, "You don't make an omelet without breaking eggs." And I guess I must rub some people the wrong way who are against what I'm doing or about to do.

Compson: What aspect of the job in the faculty practice do you think is most important?

O'Brien: I think it's improving the net revenues. I've spoken with the billing clerk in the practice and she thinks the doctors could vastly improve utilization of the facility by making changes in the block scheduling, so that docs aren't allocated time slots if they're not using them effectively. Also, the reports generated by the practice could be greatly improved. I'd like to track physician productivity in dollars relative to the opportunity costs involved in their using examining room space.

Compson: Before you go, is there anything you would like to ask me about the job?

O'Brien: As a matter of fact there is. We've talked about the salary and the benefits, but if I perform as expected, what is the likelihood of a decent increase after the first year? You know I have a wife and two young children.

Compson: Well, I'd say the chances are pretty good. Dr. Bones is fair and I think would be generous if the practice results improved significantly. (She turns off the tape recorder).

Brass: He seems like a fine candidate.

Salvatore Sorrentino

Compson (to Brass): Sal Sorrentino is the next candidate. Sal is 27. He is presentable, although he dresses a bit on the flashy side—fast talking and enthusiastic. When I spoke to his reference, Dr. Plotkin of the neighborhood health center, he recommended Sal highly for the position. He said that Sal was idealistic, energetic, and pleasant. If there was any weakness, Dr. Plotkin thought that Dr. Bones should make sure that Sal realizes that he must check with him before initiating any policy or taking policy action. Nothing serious. I asked him what he meant, but Dr. Plotkin couldn't remember anything specific other than Sorrentino's setting up an appointment for Plotkin to talk with a community group about opening a satellite health center without clearing with Plotkin first. But this had been during his first few months on the job, and Dr. Plotkin repeated that he recommended Sal highly. (Compson plays a tape of the interview.)

Compson: Sal, can you tell me in a few words something about your background and experience?

Sorrentino: Yes, I can. I was a political science major at City University, then I got involved with various community groups. While working with St. Angelo's Church, I was active in trying to improve the availability of maternal and child health services to the Latino population, as a result of which I met the assistant director for community relations at the neighborhood health center. We talked and really hit it off. We were both vitally concerned with helping people in difficulty, and in making a bureaucracy work in helping patients rather than merely serving the needs of the staff. Well, I guess he liked me a lot, and before long I was offered a position as administrative assistant. After working for two years at the neighborhood health center, I was fortunate in securing a scholarship so that I could attend the City graduate program in health policy and management.

Compson: And what would you say, Sal, was your greatest accomplishment at the neighborhood health center?

Sorrentino: Well, one of the things I am proudest of is the community health fair I planned and organized. We involved community groups of all ethnic and work-related backgrounds, and got the health professionals to man the booths at the fair. We worked with business corporations to get prizes and literature, on proper nutrition, for example. We conducted screening examinations for eye problems, and provided TB (tuberculosis) and Pap tests. We followed up on all patients who needed help after the fair was over. The fair was well attended and many people learned for the first time about the services the center had to offer. Of course, there are a lot of other things I accomplished, such as implementing a new billing system at the satellite of the neighborhood health center.

Compson: Tell me more about that.

Sorrentino: It wasn't so much really. But we needed to get more information than we were getting about patients coming for service. We had to make an effort to collect from those patients who could pay something, and to have records that were suitable for reporting purposes. It was hard to implement because the staff was more interested in the patients getting service than in collecting the money.

Compson: I see. In the position we have been talking about, what do you think would be your greatest asset?

Sorrentino: Well, I see the highest priority for the group is that of attracting more patients. As my father told me, the way you make money in a business is primarily by increasing revenue rather than cutting back on expenses. I think the practice could improve rapport with patients and make changes in the suite so that the setting would be more attractive and comfortable for them. I think the practice would probably need an attractive brochure. The waiting area should be spruced up. I think the patient should know in advance how much services will cost. I'd like to devote part of my time to developing relationships with HMOs and managed care plans to increase referrals. I think the practice could benefit by extending the hours of operation. I think the suite should at least be open on Saturday mornings and one evening besides.

Compson: That sounds like an excellent idea. I've been pushing for Saturday hours also, but we aren't using our full capacity during the week as it is now. Another question, Sal, what do you think would be your greatest liability, if any, if we were to offer and you were to accept the position?

Sorrentino: I don't know. I want to get things done in a hurry, I guess. I'm eager for results. Maybe I have a tendency to move a little too fast. Not really. It's hard to talk of one's faults. I really think that I can, would be able to do the job perfectly well, and I'd like the opportunity to do so. I'm not always that good at following through on all the little details of an operation. But I'm excellent at working with people who will see to all the details.

Compson: I'm a little sorry to hear that because I think a lot of details are involved in this work.

Sorrentino: I didn't mean to say that I didn't like detail work or that I wasn't good at it. I would just say that it's a relative weakness—I really prefer the other kind of work I was describing rather than doing the billing clerk's work for her.

Compson: I see. What do you think is the most important aspect of the job we've been talking about in terms of the work that needs to be done?

Sorrentino: I guess first you have to get all your systems working properly, use of the suite, billing and reporting; and I think next the most important thing is to increase revenues. I think part of Dr. Bones's plan for the department is for the faculty practice to finance research by supporting faculty salaries that wouldn't otherwise be available.

Compson: You're right there. Is there anything now you want to ask me about the job, before you go up and talk to Dr. Bones?

Sorrentino: Two things really. First, what kind of person is Dr. Bones to work for? And, second, do you think there are good opportunities in management to further advance from this position?

Compson: In answer to your first question, I think Dr. Bones is an excellent person to work for, so long as you produce for him. He's loyal, gives you enough autonomy. Perhaps my only complaint is that it is sometimes difficult to see him, or rather that I have felt that he is such a busy man that I don't want to bother him with things I would like to discuss. I have recommended to him that he appoint another physician within the department as head of the faculty practice, at which time access to Dr. Bones will be less difficult. As to your second question, yes, I think the medical center is a large employer of people like yourself and that you can make a lot of useful contacts here. Also I feel that ambulatory care is the place to be in healthcare management in the nineties. (She turns off the tape.)

Brass: Well, these first two candidates have quite contrasting backgrounds. Yet it seems clear to me that either of them might do a perfectly respectable job, although of course the outcomes resulting from their work might be quite different.

Marcia Rabin

Compson (to Brass): Yes, that's so. The third candidate is Marcia Rabin. Marcia is 24, attractive and peppy. Les Carson, director of human resources at Partners Nursing Homes recommended her highly for the position. Ms. Rabin was director of human resources at the Brant unit. Carson said she was hardworking, gets along well with professional and nonprofessional staff. If there is any fault to find with her, Carson said it was that Rabin takes her work too seriously, drives herself too hard, and then may be absent for a few days, largely because she has difficulty in determining priorities. But Carson stressed that Rabin has performed very well on all the big jobs that he has given her to do, that she was reliable and competent. (Compson plays a tape of the interview.)

Compson: Ms. Rabin, can you tell me in a few words something about your background and experience?

Rabin: Certainly, I guess, you don't want me to go back to high school, but I was president of my student government at Suburban High. In college I majored in psychology, and for a while I thought I would like to be a psychologist. But my father works in a hospital; he is director of housekeeping at Sisters Hospital, and he encouraged me to go into healthcare management. After attending the City graduate program, I worked for two years as director of human resources at the Brant unit. Previously they didn't have a department of human resources, but when the nursing home merged with Partners, a department was established. I had worked a year previously in the department at Partners under Mr. Carson's supervision.

Compson: What would you say was your greatest accomplishment as director of human resources?

Rabin: Really, I think it was my ability to fill all the entry-level jobs, or rather to keep filling them. Also, we started and finished a job classification system under my supervision, and inaugurated an annual pay increment schedule that I think worked more fairly than the previous system. I think my real accomplishment was in legitimating the department of human resources in the nursing home where such a department had never existed before. This meant being able to service other departments and to accomplish jobs for them that used to take up a lot of their time or that they couldn't do as well before.

Compson: That sounds interesting. In terms of the present position with Dr. Bones, what would you say was your greatest asset?

Rabin: I don't know exactly how to answer that question. My first response would be to say I like and am good at doing systems work—creating order out of chaos, and working effectively with people so that they feel it is their system, not something that I pushed on them. Of course, this is difficult to do, because in my case, the departments had to accept the human resources system we established; it's the only way to do things as part of a large organization. But at least the pacing and some of the details were left to them, and first we proved that we really could be of help to them.

Compson: And what, if you'll pardon my asking, would you say is your greatest liability?

Rabin: Well, if you must know, Ms. Compson, I'm not aggressive enough. Sometimes I think my efforts aren't properly appreciated, and I don't push myself to the front the way some people do. I work hard and I work well and it annoys me, sometimes more than it should, that others who don't work so hard and do so well push themselves forward and move ahead faster.

Compson: What aspect of the job, as I have tried to outline it to you, would you say is the most important, I mean at this time in the history of the faculty practice?

Rabin: I think you have to set up more clearly defined ways of doing things, *systems* if you prefer the word. I noted in the materials that you shared with me that your collection rate isn't what it should be; and that your utilization of examining rooms is well below capacity also. I don't think that this kind of systems work is so different from my work in human resources, plus I have taken a few courses in quantitative analysis and feel pretty comfortable with numbers.

Compson: Are there any questions that you would like to ask me?

Rabin: Well, one question is how have the physicians, most of them men, related to having a woman in this position; and second, when can you let me know if you are offering me the job. I have been offered a job as assistant director of human resources at King Hospitals, and although they aren't pressing me that hard, I would like to be able to tell them something soon.

Compson: With regard to the first question: sure, some of the physicians don't give you the respect as a manager that you would like to have, but I don't know to what extent this has to do with my being a woman. I think being a woman also has its advantages, with some of the docs. I think it will take about a month for Dr. Bones to decide on a candidate. I can't tell you what you should say to the King people. You are one of the four candidates whom I am sending on to see Dr. Bones. (She turns off the tape.)

Bonnie Goldsmith

Compson (to Brass): I don't know, Tim. Permit me to introduce our last candidate, Bonnie Goldsmith. She dresses conservatively and gives the impression of a modest, unassuming, kindly, young woman of 27. Her boss, Dr. Muldoon, who recently left the DHHS, recommended Bonnie very highly for the position we have in mind. He described Bonnie as hard working, modest, and reliable. He said that Bonnie gets along well with people. If she has any weakness, Bonnie lacks drive and has a tendency to check with her boss about every little thing. However, Dr. Muldoon says that once a task is clearly outlined, Bonnie takes the bit between her teeth and doesn't let up. He praised highly Bonnie's staff work on the recent Task Force on the Aging Report. (She plays a tape of the interview.)

Compson: Bonnie, can you tell me a few words about your background and experience?

Goldsmith: Yes, I was a zoology major at City University. Originally, I wanted to be a physician. In fact, I attended medical school for one year, then decided it just wasn't for me. My father's a psychiatrist. I didn't know what I wanted to do. I don't know why but I thought that working in a hospital admitting department might be interesting, and I did that for a while. The administrator is a good friend of my father's, and he talked to me and convinced me to apply to City University's graduate program in health policy and management. Back in school I really enjoyed courses in continuous quality improvement, information systems, and statistics. A whole new world opened up to me, although I must confess I had a bit of difficulty with some of the heavy reading and writing courses. After graduation, I was fortunate to get a position with the Department of Health and Human Services. My father's connections helped there. I've been working for two years at DHHS doing mostly staff work, learning a lot, and I've done quite a bit of traveling.

Compson: What would you say has been your greatest accomplishment at DHHS?

Goldsmith: I would say it was the staff work I did on the President's Task Force on the Aging. I went into a lot of nursing homes and other chronic care institutions and saw what a lousy deal most of our aged get. It isn't so much this way in Europe, which I visited a couple of years ago with my father. In Europe, the homes are more like residences and fewer people go into homes. When they do go, they can take their furniture with them, and it doesn't cost as much.

Compson: What kind of solutions did you come up with?

Goldsmith: Well, it's a pretty difficult problem. I mean the part about making it possible not to have to institutionalize the elderly. I guess there are tax incentives which could be passed to allow people to keep their relatives at home. Also, more people should be able to bring their relatives into homes for day care activities, and to institutionalize them for a week or two each year if necessary, either because the aged member of the household is sick, or because other members of the household want a rest. Of course, we need better regulation of nursing homes to set standards for care and to establish closer relations between homes and hospitals.

Compson: I see. What do you think would be your greatest asset in the position that exists here within the department of medicine?

Goldsmith: I don't know. Perhaps it's my ability to get along with and to understand the needs and problems of the medical profession. I don't have a big ego. I like analytical work, solving operations problems, and I think I'm pretty persistent in trying to solve them.

Compson: And your greatest liability?

Goldsmith: Well, some people think I'm not aggressive enough. I don't know what this means, really, unless it is forcing your opinions on others. I guess I'm not a great innovator, and I don't like to work that much. I mean I work hard, but I don't want work to be an obsession, like it is for my father. I mean that I'm married, with a nice husband and a young son, and I want to enjoy my work and do well, but I also want to enjoy my family. I guess you could call it a lack of ambition. But I think this country needs more people like me, people whose satisfaction comes from a job well done rather than striving for money, status, and power. I'm intellectually committed to group practice as a better way to deliver healthcare, and I'd like to do my part to see that primary care is improved in this country. So this may be a liability or an asset, I don't know.

Compson: I'm not sure either. But certainly if you do the job well, what you say makes sense. Well enough of that, what aspects of the job strike you as most important?

Goldsmith: Well, I don't know. Certainly , the practice has to be organized systematically, and billing has to be improved. I'd like to track these processes scientifically, see what the standards are and should be, track the variance from standards by analyzing all the steps in these processes, and then work with all the individuals involved from physicians to receptionists in improving these systems. This might require a number of meetings, and I don't know how feasible such meetings would be because of people's time requirements. There are a few questions I would like to ask you.

Compson: Please go ahead.

Goldsmith: My first question is do you think the faculty practice is going to grow? The second is incidental, but I would like to know more about the benefits, such as tuition remission, as I was thinking of furthering my education at City, perhaps taking some more courses in statistical analysis.

Compson: I think the faculty practice will continue to grow. Space is our key constraint now, and the medical center will have to figure out better how we are going to deal with managed care. Also, should we eventually combine the faculty practice plans in the various departments into one multidisciplinary group practice that is also in the managed care business? Of course this all has to be squared with the department's ambitious goals in teaching and research. Sometimes, despite the excellent reputation of the medical center and the quality of its leadership, I wonder if we can possibly excel in all these different areas as well as in all of the leading areas of clinical medicine. With respect to your second question, yes, I believe tuition remission for such purposes is available, although I don't see where you will have the time to fit everything in with the demands of this job which are quite considerable and with your family obligations. (She turns off the tape.)

Brass: Well, Sandy, now all you have to do is tell Dr. Bones whom you recommend for the job.

Compson: I need to sleep on it. This assignment has given me more problems than I bargained for, but that's the joy of working, isn't it, Tim, solving these problems?

Brass: I agree with you there. Sorry, but I've got to leave now. I want to think about this some more and I'll give you my opinion tomorrow.

The Associate Director and the Controllers

Anthony R. Kovner

Fortunately for Jim Joel, he didn't lose his temper often. Otherwise, he might not have been able to function as associate director of the Morris Health Care Program of the Nathan D. Wise Medical Center (see Illustration 2.1, the Organization Chart). But now, he had become so enraged at the Morris program controller, Percy Oram, that he had to concentrate hard to keep from yelling. Joel had just been informed by Felix Schwartzberg, an assistant director, that the accounting department was not collecting cash from the billing assistants in the family health units as previously agreed. Oram did not usually keep in close enough touch with Joel concerning his actions. But in any case, Joel knew his own reaction was excessive. An aspiring health services executive did not throw a tantrum, which is what Joel now felt like doing.

Joel was 30 years old, ambitious, a recent graduate from Ivy University's Master in Health Care Administration program. Before returning to school, he had worked as a registered representative on Wall Street, where he had found the work remunerative but uninteresting. The director of the Ivy program, Dr. Leon Russell, assumed the post of director of the Nathan D. Wise Medical Center in 1966. Joel, one of his best students, asked to join Russell toward the end of that year, and he was hired shortly thereafter as an assistant hospital administrator. The Nathan D. Wise Medical Center is located in New York City and comprises three large programs: the Nathan D. Wise Hospital, the Lennox Rehabilitation Center, and the Morris Health Care Program. The hospital and the rehabilitation center are owned by the Wise Medical Center, but the Morris

Illustration 2.1　Organization Chart: Nathan D. Wise Medical Center

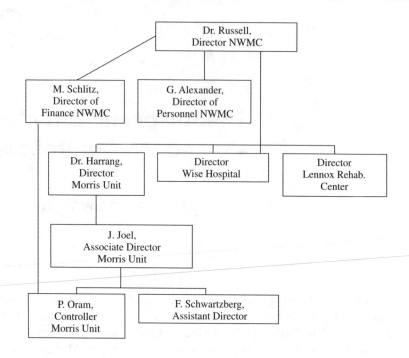

Health Care Program is operated by the Wise Medical Center under contract with the City of New York and is located in a city-owned facility.

Russell had been impressed with his former student's drive and promise, and had originally created a job for Joel. This included half-time as a staff assistant at Wise Hospital, and half-time as an evaluator at the Morris Unit, where new methods of delivering ambulatory medical care were being developed and demonstrated. However, the director of the Morris Unit, Dr. Lawrence White, had resigned to become commissioner of health of a midwestern city, and six months later his associate director, Mr. Philip Bright, had announced his intention to resign to join White. By March 1967, Russell had already hired a replacement for White, Dr. Miller Harrang, a 45-year-old physician, who had previously been medical director of the Ochs Ambulatory Care Unit in another part of New York State. Since Joel was not being fully utilized at Wise Hospital, although he had performed capably whatever he had been asked to do, Russell decided to offer him the position of associate director of the Morris Unit.

Joel felt ambivalent regarding Russell's offer. He knew he would take the position, even before requesting a night to think it over, but at the same time he had certain reservations. Joel was enjoying his work at the hospital.

He had submitted an in-depth plan for increasing efficiency of the operating room, which had been enthusiastically accepted by the medical staff executive committee, and he was just starting an evaluation of patient transport in the hospital. His key interest was implementation of his master's thesis on nurse staffing. Joel believed that by assigning rooms to patients on the basis of their nursing needs, one-third fewer registered nurses would be required. Joel wished to be director of a large general hospital within ten years. He wasn't sure how working at the Morris Unit would advance him toward that goal, nor how comfortable he would feel working in a facility serving the poor in a slum section of the city.

However, after taking the job, Joel found before long that he liked working at the Morris Unit immensely. Morris was rapidly expanding. In the last year, the number of physician visits had increased 25 percent to 215,000. Through a generous grant from the Office of Economic Opportunity (OEO), the budget had increased from $1.5 million to $2.5 million. Joel worked 65–70 hours a week. There was so much to do. He liked Harrang, his present boss, and he liked the people who worked at Morris. The atmosphere was busy and informal, a nice change of pace from the Wise Hospital where things happened more slowly. Dramatic change was the norm at Morris, whether this was conversion of the medical and pediatric clinics to family health units, or confrontations with a community health council resulting in increased participation in policymaking by the poor. There was no formal division of responsibility between Harrang and Joel. Harrang spent most of his time in community relations (time-consuming and frustrating), in individual conversations with members of the medical staff at Morris, and in working out problems with the Wise Hospital. Harrang also took responsibility for certain medical units such as the emergency room, obstetrics-gynecology (ob-gyn), and psychiatry. Joel's primary responsibility lay in the area of staff activities such as finance, personnel, and purchasing. He also supervised several departments or units, including laboratory, x-ray, pharmacy, dental, housekeeping, and maintenance. Responsibility for the family health units was shared by the two top administrators.

Under the former top administrators, White and Bright, the Morris Unit had been run as a unit independent from the Wise Hospital. The unit was decentralized, with departments such as laboratory and internal medicine handling their own personnel and often their own purchasing. It was Russell's wish to create a more integrated medical center, and Joel saw an important part of his job as creating staff departments (such as personnel and purchasing) and upgrading these functions through the help of medical center experts.

When Joel arrived, the controller's department consisted of four individuals: Bill Connor, the controller, who promptly resigned (Joel never met this individual whom he was told had personal problems of an unspecified nature); Peter Stavrogin, an industrious bookkeeper, who was a 55-year-old East European refugee with a limited knowledge of English; a payroll clerk; and a secretary. This was the staff for an organization of over 400 employees that was funded by five different agencies under five different contracts. The accounting department had heavy personnel responsibilities as well in spring 1967, at least so far as payroll was concerned, since no personnel department as such existed. One of the first things Joel did was to hire Connor's replacement. In doing so—and to conform with Russell's policy of an integrated medical center—Joel enlisted the help of the medical center staff: Milton Schlitz, the director of financial affairs, and Grover Alexander, the director of personnel. Alexander volunteered to place the ads and check the references of applicants for the controller position, and Schlitz suggested that he screen the applicants. The best three or four would then be reviewed by Joel and Harrang who, between them, would select the new controller. Joel was pleased with this arrangement, although he thought the recommended salary for the position was too low. He agreed to go along, however, based on the recommendations of Alexander and Schlitz, who had considerably more experience in these matters.

However, because of what Schlitz and Alexander believed to be a shortage of qualified accountants, and the undesirable location of Morris, they found only two prospective applicants. Albert Fodor, a 55-year-old certified public accountant (CPA), with no hospital experience but good references was the obvious first choice to be Morris's new controller. Fodor was pleasant and industrious. It took him six months to learn the job. Fodor then resigned, citing that the tremendous pressure and workload were too great for a man of his years. The payroll clerk also resigned at this time for a higher-paying job at another hospital.

During the next three months, Joel employed three new billing clerks as well as a personnel assistant and a purchasing agent. Most of the accounting department's work, which would have been done by the controller, was performed by Joel and Stavrogin. Joel handled the budgetary aspects and Stavrogin the accounting aspects. This system was unsatisfactory, however, from the standpoint of Schlitz and Joel, both of whom wished Joel to spend less time troubleshooting financial problems and more time on the programmatic aspects of the job. Also, Joel wanted to conduct and supervise a variety of special studies for contract purposes and cost comparisons, an undertaking hardly feasible under the present setup.

So Joel went back to Schlitz and Alexander, insisting that the salary for the controller job be raised $3,000 per year because of the complexity of the job and the distance from Schlitz's direct supervision. Schlitz agreed reluctantly; he knew he would have to raise salaries or face morale problems in the accounting department at Wise Hospital.

After an intensive advertising program, eight to ten candidates had been screened by Schlitz, and three candidates were sent to Joel and Harrang. Perry Oram seemed clearly the best. Oram was 40 years old, without a CPA but with solid accounting experience in a medium-sized business firm. Oram had no hospital or healthcare experience. Schlitz and Joel did not feel that such experience was necessary for the job, although, of course, they would have preferred it. Oram was physically attractive, well-dressed, married, with no children. He said he was interested in advancing himself in the expanding hospital field. Joel went over the Fodor experience with Oram, stressing the work pressures. Oram responded that he was looking for a job where he would have more autonomy, where he was in charge and responsible, and where he knew he would be rewarded (or blamed) based on his performance. Of course, he would like to spend a lot of time at first learning the ropes with Schlitz. Joel told Oram he would let him know later that week if the job was his. Afterward, Joel and Harrang agreed that Oram was the best of the three candidates. However, Harrang had a vague feeling of unease. Oram seemed too good, too qualified for the job. Independently, Schlitz also agreed that Oram was the best of the three candidates, and that Oram was a promising candidate indeed. Alexander checked Oram's reference which confirmed the high opinion of Schlitz and Joel. Oram was then offered the job as controller of the Morris Unit, and he accepted.

From Joel's point of view, things went fairly well at first, perhaps because Joel was busy with other matters and because Oram was spending a lot of time at Wise Hospital with Schlitz. The first sign of trouble was the lateness of the monthly statement that Joel had instituted and required. The statement included detailed categories of departmental costs, comparing costs (Joel hoped eventually to compare costs with performance as well) for this month, last month, and this month last year, as well as cumulative totals for this year. Joel had reviewed with Oram how he wanted the statement done (in what categories), with a cover sheet that would suggest the reasons for any large variances. Oram agreed to furnish such a report, but one month after the month in question, Joel still hadn't received it. When asked, Oram said that he was too busy, and that he was working on it. When the statement finally did arrive on Joel's desk, there was no cover letter about variances, and there were large variances caused by sloppy accounting (items in one category last year, for instance, that were in another this year, causing large discrepancies). Even some of the amounts in the categories were incorrect, salaries of certain individuals not having been counted in the proper categories. Joel, patiently but with irritation, explained that this was not what he wanted. He told Oram why he wanted what he wanted, and when he wanted the report—15 days after the end of the month. Timeliness, he emphasized, was especially important because, although the city contract remained at the same sum every year, changes in the OEO budget had to be individually approved by Washington, and OEO funds had to be spent by the year's end. This meant that a lot of shuffling had to be done (e.g., transfer of city positions because of increased salary costs to the OEO budget) based on correct information. Oram apologized and agreed to improve performance.

At the same time, Joel had begun to hear complaints about Oram from other staff members. Linda Lee, the personnel assistant, and Felix Schwartzberg, the assistant director, complained about his rudeness, arrogance, and insensitivity to the poor—like his repeated statements about "welfare chiselers." Such terminology was at odds with the philosophy of the unit. When changes in employee paychecks had to be made because of supervisory mistakes or because of inadequate notice concerning an employee's vacation, Oram reluctantly did the extra work. However, he warned those involved, without clearing this with Joel, that eventually checks would not be issued on this basis.

Joel had been approached by Oram two weeks previously about a personal matter. Oram explained that he had to come to work an hour and a half late twice a week because of an appointment with his psychiatrist. The psychiatrist couldn't see him before or after work, and he hoped Joel would be sympathetic. Oram was willing to stay late to make up the time. Joel said he wanted to think it over before responding. Joel then discussed Oram's situation with Schlitz and Harrang. They all agreed that they would have liked to have known this before Oram was hired, but that if the work was done and he made up the time, it would be permitted. It was agreed that Joel would check occasionally in the accounting office, which was located in a separate building a block away from the health services facility, to see if Oram was indeed putting in the extra time.

For about the next six months, Oram's performance remained essentially the same. The cover letter was superficial, and the statements were late and often contained mistakes. (The statements did, however, eventually arrive and were eventually corrected.) The special studies requested of Oram were done late and Joel often had to redo them. In checking up on Oram, Joel never found him in the office after 5:00 p.m., but he did not check every day. The routine work of the accounting department was being done effectively, but this had been the case before the current situation with Oram, when no controller had been present. Oram had added another clerk, and Joel suspected that Stavrogin was still performing much of the supervisory work as he had been previous to Oram's arrival. Joel was not happy. He discussed the situation with Harrang, who agreed that the statements were less than acceptable. Harrang told Joel to do as he liked, but to clear it first with Schlitz.

Soon after, Joel went to Wise Hospital to discuss Oram with Schlitz. Schlitz, a CPA, had been controller of Wise Hospital, now Wise Medical Center, for 27 years. Schlitz was talkative but often vague, hard-working, basically conservative, and oriented primarily to the needs of Wise Hospital (at least in Joel's opinion) rather than to the Medical Center at large. This was reflected in the allocation of overhead in the Morris contracts (e.g., administrative time allocated was greater than that actually provided) and in the high price of direct services, such as laboratory, performed for Morris by the hospital. More importantly, Schlitz saw his job almost exclusively as worrying about "the bottom line"—whether the hospital or the Morris Unit ran a deficit or broke even—rather than in terms of performance relative to costs. Nevertheless, Joel thought he had established a cordial relationship with Schlitz, and their discussion about Oram was indeed cordial for the most part. Schlitz agreed that Oram's performance left something to be desired. He was particularly unhappy about the time Oram put in. On the other hand, Schlitz felt that the Morris Unit was in good financial shape and that there was nothing to worry about. In view of the experience with the previous controller, Fodor, Schlitz wondered if indeed they could find a better man for the salary. Schlitz urged that they talk to Oram together, but said that he would go along with whatever Joel wanted to do.

Acting on Schlitz's recommendation, Joel set up a meeting with Schlitz, Oram, and Harrang to discuss his dissatisfactions. During the course of the meeting Joel did admit that the monthly statements were improving, but only after extensive prodding. Oram remarked that the reason for this meeting surprised him; that he had thought, on the basis of previous meetings with Joel and Schlitz, that they were pleased with his work. He then asked, in fact, to be included in more top-level policy meetings, as he felt that controllers should be part of the top management group. Oram said he felt isolated, which resulted in part from the location of the accounting department in a separate building. Joel responded that he would welcome Oram's participation in policy meetings after the work of the accounting department had been sufficiently upgraded, and that Oram would be kept informed and invited to all meetings that concerned his department.

Returning to the Morris facility, Joel discussed his perplexity with Harrang. Actually, he asserted, he did not understand what was going on here. Oram never gave him what he wanted. He had no way of knowing how busy Oram actually was. Lately, Oram had said that he couldn't produce certain studies by the stipulated dates because he was busy doing work for Schlitz or attending meetings at the hospital with Schlitz and the controllers of the other units of the medical center.

Harrang replied that he believed that Schlitz was indeed responsible in part for Oram's lack of responsiveness. Schlitz had probably told Oram not to listen to Joel but to do what he, Schlitz, recommended, since Oram's salary and benefits were largely determined by Schlitz rather than by Joel. Schlitz didn't want the accounting department at Morris to use more sophisticated techniques relating to the hospital because this would reflect badly on Schlitz. Moreover, Schlitz wanted his "own man" at the Morris Unit so that the hospital benefited in all transactions with Morris (e.g., there should be enough slack in the city budget to meet any contingency, with as many staff as possible switched to the OEO budget).

Joel had to agree with Harrang's observation. But on the other hand, Harrang had became increasingly bitter toward Russell over the last six months. This concerned a variety of matters, most specifically Harrang's salary. Harrang was working much harder than he had bargained for at Morris, and he didn't feel he was getting the money or the credit he deserved. Nevertheless, Joel did think that Schlitz might be part of the problem; he had never been particularly impressed with Schlitz.

Several weeks later, a new state regulation was passed stating that for city agencies to collect under Medicaid, all efforts must be made to collect from those who, by state edict, could afford to pay. This was in conflict with Morris's philosophy of providing free service to all who said they couldn't pay, and there was much opposition to implementation of the policy by the professionals at Morris. The professional staff felt that no special effort should be made to collect from those who had formerly received free services. Oram disagreed with this philosophy and said that Morris should make every effort to collect.

When it came to implementing collections, Oram requested that the registration staff who were to collect the money should be part of his department, or that a separate cashier's office should be set up on the first floor of the health facility. Otherwise his department didn't wish to be involved. Schwartzberg, the assistant director in charge of registration, argued that the registration staff should continue as part of the family health units because of other duties, that no space was available on the first floor for a cashier's office, and that it was not fair to patients to make them stand in two lines, as they would have to under Oram's arrangement, before seeing a health professional. Joel and Harrang sided with Schwartzberg and discussed with Oram a plan under which he would be responsible for the cash collection aspects of the registrar's work. It was agreed that Oram would devise, within a week, a plan for implementation. After two weeks, Schwartzberg reported to Joel that Oram had not devised a plan and was unwilling to cooperate with the plan Schwartzberg and the chief registrar had devised.

Joel pounded his desk. What concerned him was not so much this specific matter, which he knew he would resolve, but what to do in general with Oram.

Joel was working Saturday mornings with a militant community group over next year's OEO budget and was still working 60–65 hours per week. He knew that it was his job to decide. He didn't think Oram's performance would improve unless Schlitz agreed with Joel's priorities and, even in that event, sufficient improvement was unlikely. On the other hand, Joel did not look forward to hiring a fourth controller in the two years he had worked at Morris. Moreover, the routine work of the accounting department was being performed to the satisfaction of Schlitz. Joel decided to go for a walk by the river and make his decision.

Short Case A

Nowhere Job

David Melman

John Ernest works for a young and growing healthcare company. The company has been successfully developing a market niche by contracting with colleges and universities to manage and operate their campus health centers. Ernest has been hired to develop the operational structure of a new product that will connect the managed care health insurance coverage of the students with their campus health center. This new product will result in cost savings and superior service delivery. It is a new concept in the industry and, while Ernest does not have significant healthcare experience, he does have a great deal of energy and enthusiasm and is expected to learn on the job.

Ernest is not given a formal job description. He is verbally given a list of performance objectives, but these objectives are changed without his input and without detailed new objectives put in their place. Ernest's work environment is unusual in that he mostly works out of a home office, with occasional trips to the corporate office 70 miles away. Ernest is told that he will report to the corporate medical director, who is located in Miami, 1,200 miles away. Communication is made by telephone, fax, and e-mail.

Ernest makes progress in achieving organizational objectives but is facing obstacles in terms of his isolation from others in the company. He is not informed of changes in project objectives, nor of the underlying reasons for these changes. Ernest finds that this isolation limits his ability to grow and contribute because he is unable to describe his company's needs accurately to outside vendors without being so informed himself.

Ernest asks to have a formal job description and stated performance objectives based on the format suggested by a human resources consultant hired by the company. He receives no response. He is asked to complete the contracts with several outside vendors he has negotiated. Ernest is told he now reports to an outside consultant who has been hired to help coordinate technical operations, including information systems. This outside consultant tells Ernest not to proceed with these contracts the very day after the CEO has told him to complete them.

Ernest attempts to contribute to the sales and marketing efforts of his company by proposing that the company sponsor an institute at a prestigious university, and he wants to contribute his time and energy to make this project a success. He is told it is a good idea, but the vice president of sales and marketing does not keep his commitment to respond to Ernest's proposal. Ernest sends reminders and continues to develop the idea with the university. He is trying to expand his job responsibilities to include business development but needs the support of others in his organization to make a meaningful contribution.

Case Questions

- What should Ernest do?
- What are the risks to Ernest?
- How could Ernest have anticipated these problems before accepting his current position?
- What should be Ernest's priorities in evaluating an alternative career opportunity? Why?

Short Case B

Manager Morale at Uptown Hospital

Anthony R. Kovner

Date: April 1995

To: CEO Martin Dexter

From: Director of Human Resources, Paula Long

In talking about our management development program with several partici-pants, I received the following feedback which I think is serious and urgent enough to bring to your attention:

1. Morale is very low because of delayed program development, no allowance for overtime or per diems, and the resultant squeeze on management.
2. The hospital suffers from lack of supervisory staff, inadequate sys-tems support, lack of trust among employees and managers, and a lack of a forum for communication upward.
3. The hospital provides a lot of substandard care, doesn't look nice, and is not "user-friendly." There are too many employees who don't "carry their load" and who are nasty.

4. The "word" for many potential users in the minority community we serve is not to go Uptown but rather to go to St. Stephen or Washington Hospitals.

5. Top management has not communicated to middle managers the strategic plan. There are no open lines of communication nor is there any shared management philosophy.

6. Good things and accomplishments by small groups aren't recognized or appreciated.

7. There is no feeling that morale will improve if financial performance improves.

8. Managers and department heads are afraid to fire someone they can't replace.

9. People are worried about their jobs.

10. No one trusts the message of the relationship with our teaching affiliate.

I have several ideas about what we should do about this, but I wanted to send this off to you right away while my thoughts further simmer.

Case Questions

- What should CEO Dexter do in receiving Paula Long's memo?
- How could such conditions have occurred at Uptown Hospital?
- What constraints and opportunities does CEO Dexter face in implementing your recommendations?
- How can CEO Dexter overcome constraints and take advantage of the opportunities?

Part **II**

Control

Introduction

What large managed care systems have in common, whether they be Intermountain Health Care, Columbia HCA, Kaiser Permanente, or Henry Ford Health System (to name only a few), is a clearly perceived need, backed by a commitment to spend substantial funds, to improve their computer-based management and clinical information systems, that is, their control system. This information is to be used not to centralize power at corporate headquarters, but rather to help professionals and practitioners in the system improve the quality of services provided and to lower costs.

In order to develop a comprehensive control system, the following elements are necessary: performance expectations to set performance guidelines; an information system to measure performance; control auspices to evaluate performance compared to expectations; an incentive system to influence producer performance; and coordinated phasing, to minimize dysfunctions of the controlling auspice.[1]

If, as Peter Drucker says, "the basic problem of service institutions is not high cost but lack of effectiveness,"[2] performance expectations in health services organizations must be defined in terms of goal attainment instead of increased budget allocations. The traditional approach to control when output measures are available, as in automobile production, is to relate capital and operational costs to unit standards of production. In healthcare, costs are usually related to process activities; therefore, a control system sensitive to cost must include some assurance of quality, since cost control does not inherently consider output quality. Consider, therefore, what the performance expectations are in the three cases in this section: "Healthier Babies in Twin Falls, Idaho," "Klee Hospital," and "Physician Specialists in Inpatient Care."

An information system includes the techniques for gathering, recording, summarizing, and disseminating data. It also includes evaluating the information system itself: the relevance and processing of data collected, the reports generated relative to the performance expectations of the controlling auspice, and the quality and cost of the system itself. What kinds of information are the managers of the three organizations in these cases using to make decisions? What kinds of information do they require for effective decision making?

In addition, who establishes performance expectations in these three organizations? Who takes responsibility for assuming that the information system is effective and efficient? Who monitors performance and takes corrective action when appropriate? And who establishes the systems procedures necessary to contrast actual performance with relevant performance expectations?

An explicitly communicated incentive framework is fundamental to an effective control system. In healthcare, the absence of output standards means that incentives must be structured on surrogate measures of output, such as the type and quantity of patients and the type and volume of procedures performed. Effective reorienting of provider performance can result if incentives are structured on the same factors for which performance expectations exist and for which data are collected. In the three cases, consider what incentives underlie the current and future decisions of the key participants.

Coordination of phasing is the process of keeping the performance of the control auspice in line with provider and customer expectations—not insisting on more than the producers are able or willing to perform and not promising to accomplish more than the principals in the organization can actually perform. Consider to what extent the managers in these cases are realistic in their expectations and their promises, or how they should have behaved.

The three cases here present very different problems of control.

Twin Falls is recognized as a leader in applying the concepts of continuous quality improvement (CQI) both within their hospital and in the community they serve. Three pillars of CQI are customer mindedness, statistical mindedness, and organizational transformation. These pillars relate to the three questions that underlie their goal to make Twin Falls the healthiest community in the country. Why do we do what we do? (Does this meet customer needs?) How do we know it works? (How do we understand and measure the process and the outcomes of care?) How can we do it better? (How do we go about creating a learning organization?) For another view of Twin Falls see the article of McEachern et al.[3]

Both the "Klee Hospital" and the "Physician Specialists in Inpatient Care" cases are concerned with creating ways to improve inpatient care. One focuses on a solution based on an information system and the other on contracting with a physician to improve care. All three cases can be considered in the context of continuous quality improvement.

Case Questions

Healthier Babies in Twin Falls, Idaho
- What is the process that leads to healthy babies as viewed by the Twin Falls team?
- Who is served by this process?
- How would one measure improvement in the process and outcome?
- What needs to be done to change the organization of care in order to keep improving this process?
- What should the team do next?

Klee Hospital
- What are the problems facing Sarah Wright?
- What are the causes of these problems?
- What do you think of the way Sarah Wright has addressed these problems? Would you have advised her to do anything differently?
- What do you recommend that Sarah Wright do now?
- What are some of the constraints and opportunities that face Sarah Wright in implementing your recommendations?

Physician Specialists in Inpatient Care
- What do you recommend that Dr. Conerly do with physicians in his group who do not want to visit their patients in the hospital?
- How do you recommend that Dr. Conerly assure care for the group's patients when an illness is too complicated or significant to allow for usual care by an internist who does not specialize in hospital care?
- What do you recommend that Dr. Conerly do after the meeting?
- What do you recommend that Sam Tittle, hospital medical director, do about in-hospital specialist care?
- What do you recommend that Willie Brown, associate dean of the medical school, do about physicians in ambulatory care who want to see patients only in the outpatient setting?

Notes

1. Anthony R. Kovner and Edward J. Lusk, "State Regulation of Health Care Costs," *Medical Care* 13, no. 8 (August 1975): 619–29.

2. Peter Drucker, "Managing the Public Service Institution," *The Public Interest* 33 (fall 1973): 43–60.
3. Edward J. McEachern, Duncan Neuhauser, Paul Miles, and John Bingham, "Managing Rural Health Care Reform," chapter 8 in *Health Systems Management: Readings and Commentary*, 6th edition, edited by Anthony R. Kovner and Duncan Neuhauser (Chicago: Health Administration Press, 1997).

Selected Bibliography

Beaulieu, Joyce E., and David E. Berry (eds.). *Rural Health Services: A Management Perspective*. Chicago: AUPHA Press/Health Administration Press, 1994.

Berwick, Donald M., A. Blanton Godfrey, and Jane Roessner. *Curing Health Care: New Strategies for Quality Improvement*. San Francisco: Jossey-Bass, 1990.

Carey, Raymond G., and Robert C. Lloyd. *Measuring Quality Improvement in Health Care*. New York, NY: Quality Resources, a Division of the Kraus Organizations Limited, 1995.

Griffith, John R. *The Well-Managed Health Care Organization*, 3rd edition. Chicago: Health Administration Press, 1992, Chapter 9.

Kovner, Anthony R., Guest Editor. (Special Issue): "Community Benefit Programs for Health Care Organizations." *The Journal of Health Administration Education* 12, no. 13 (summer 1994).

Marczynski-Music, Karen K. *Health Care Solutions: Designing Community-Based Systems That Work*. San Francisco: Jossey-Bass Publishers, 1994.

Milio, Nancy. *Engines of Empowerment: Using Information Technology to Create Healthy Communities and Challenge Public Policy*. Chicago: Health Administration Press, 1996.

Trabin, Tom (ed.). *The Computerization of Behavioral Healthcare: How to Enhance Clinical Practice, Management, and Communications*. San Francisco: Jossey-Bass Publishers, 1996.

Case 3

Healthier Babies in Twin Falls, Idaho

Dorothy Shaffer

Emily Blackwell is spending a summer in Twin Falls, Idaho learning about continuous quality improvement. She has been providing staff support for Paul Miles, MD, who chairs the hospital's project to make the area the healthiest place in America to have a baby.

Idaho, the seventh most sparsely populated state, has the lowest physician-to-population ratio in the nation (114 physicians per 100,000 people, national average 184 per 100,000).[1] There are 1,000,000 people living in the state, with 145,000 people living in Magic Valley, an agricultural-based community in south central Idaho (11,000 square miles). The Valley, composed of eight counties, has a population density of 12.2 persons per square mile (ppsm) compared to the national average of 69.4 ppsm, and two of the counties are classified as "frontier."[1] This area of Idaho is unique with its low population, lack of public transportation, and the worst low-birthweight and perinatal mortality rates in the state. In 1988, Magic Valley's low-birthweight rate was 6.6 percent with a state average of 5.1 percent. Concurrently, the perinatal mortality rate was 10.7 per 1,000 for Magic Valley and 9.2 per 1,000 for the state.[1]

Twin Falls, population 29,000, is the largest town in this eight-county region, and the city is home to the two largest hospitals in Magic Valley. The Southcentral Public Health Department is also located here. There is no managed care in the area or in the state. One of the hospitals, The Twin

The author wishes to thank Paul Miles, M.D., Duncan Neuhauser, Ph.D., and Linda Headrick, M.D. for their teaching and guidance.

Falls Clinic, with a 44-bed capacity, is under private ownership and the only hospital in Idaho that is not a member of the Idaho Hospital Association. The facility provides limited services with no general pediatrics or ob-gyn, but it does have some subspecialties unique to the area, including plastic surgery, rheumatology, and endocrinology.[2] The other hospital in Twin Falls is Magic Valley Regional Medical Center (MVRMC), a not-for-profit, county-owned hospital that serves as a secondary care institution for the eight-county region and is designated as the Medicare regional referral center. The hospital is managed by Quorum Health Resources, has a $55 million revenue, and a 165-bed capacity. There are 123 physicians with privileges at MVRMC, 80 of whom are very active. Their patient population is made up of 50 percent Medicare and 14 percent Medicaid patients.[3] Four smaller, rural hospitals are also located within this region; they are staffed by family practitioners and all are under different ownership and funding. The Department of Public Health is run by the district and serves this same eight-county region. The department has a number of outlying facilities and multiple specialty and preventive health clinics within its Twin Falls office. All of the hospitals and health services have separate visions, separate patient registrations, and separate databases. Communication between these facilities is poor, and care is often duplicated.

Within this environment, healthcare resources are scarce, difficult to gain access to, and disjointed. This is a condition not uncommon to much of America, but because Idaho has an inadequate supply of physicians and resources, the status of healthcare cannot continue to be ignored. In 1987, the hospital board at MVRMC revised their vision statement to read, "MVRMC will be a standard of excellence and cooperation in making Magic Valley the healthiest place in America." With this change, John Bingham, the hospital administrator, introduced a new way to approach healthcare in order to achieve this vision. His interests were based on the Deming Management Method,[4] but he was also influenced by both Bronowski[5] and Senge.[6] The process, labeled continuous quality improvement (CQI), emphasizes cooperation, systems thinking, and an understanding of statistical variation and human interactions within a given system. This model involves a strict reliance on data collection and analysis, while using the scientific method to institute change and improvement. Deming, an American statistician whose work was closely linked to Japan's postwar economic growth, used the above ideas to transform business management and production.[4] Bingham wanted to attempt the same transformation in healthcare.

Bingham was aware that many of these ideas were broad and difficult to initiate. Nevertheless, he was driven by two fundamental questions: "Why do we do what we do? And how do we know that what we do works?" which took him to a third question: "How can we make what we do better?"[7] His shift to quality improvement and a systems view of healthcare (Illustration 3.1) was supported by the Hospital Corporation of America (HCA), the hospital's former management group before Quorum. Magic Valley Regional Medical Center became a pilot hospital of HCA for implementing quality improvement. However, even with this support, Bingham had reservations about the change in thinking because the new approach could be perceived as another fad in healthcare reform and there was still a question whether Deming's theories could be effective or not in the healthcare industry. Regardless, he started at the top, with the hospital board, as a way to anchor these ideas first and then incorporate them into the daily functioning of the hospitals and the surrounding community.[7] He and the hospital began accomplishing this vision by addressing parts of the system, with the continual focus on restoring and improving the community's health.

During the time of this transition, the state was involved in the Idaho Perinatal Project and had been working for eight years to address the issues of perinatal morbidity and mortality. In an effort to decrease this problem, the project's goal was to standardize the equipment and training for neonatal resuscitation across the state. They successfully improved the facilities and staff training without improving the process, and the mortality rates did not improve. As mentioned, by 1988, the state's perinatal mortality rate was 9.2 per 1,000 and the low-birthweight percentage, an indicator of neonatal morbidity, was 5.1 percent which still left Idaho with the same problem it had attempted to fix.[1]

Dr. Paul Miles, a pediatrician in Twin Falls and member of the hospital board at MVRMC, was working with the Idaho Perinatal Project. Because of his close connection to Mr. Bingham and the MVRMC, he decided to apply the quality improvement theories to the ongoing perinatal project. There are

Illustration 3.1   Systems View of Healthcare

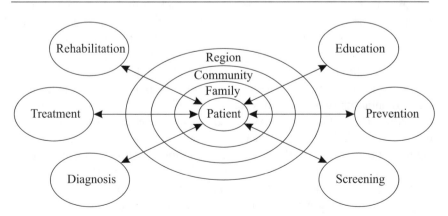

33 physicians in Magic Valley providing obstetrics care, and 20 percent of the MVRMC admissions are pregnancy related. Approximately 50 percent of the total deliveries in the area are performed at MVRMC, with the majority of high-risk newborns treated in their neonatal intensive care unit (NICU).[8]

The very high risk newborns are transferred to tertiary care centers in Boise, Idaho (130 miles west) or Salt Lake City, Utah (200 miles southeast). This eight-county district, although fully up to date with its equipment still had some of the worst outcome data, mentioned earlier, in one of the worst states. Within this region and using quality improvement guidelines, Miles realized the great opportunity that existed to better the health of pregnant women, newborns, and the community as a whole.

In Miles' thinking, the next step to take in solving the problem of perinatal morbidity and mortality in Idaho centered on the vision of making Magic Valley the healthiest place in America to have a baby and to cooperate with all of the care providers in the area. To achieve this goal, a systems approach was adopted, keeping in mind the strengths and weaknesses of the community while always keeping the patient at the focal point of care. Magic Valley Regional Medical Center, along with the Public Health Department and a few physicians, began looking at prevention and improvement along with treatment. They wanted to become proactive in their problem solving with an emphasis on continual learning and improving upon the existing model.

Formally, the continuous quality improvement (CQI) plan contains a step-by-step approach in applying the scientific method to problem solving. Initially, a problem is identified and a plan for improvement is made (the hypothesis). Then, the plan is executed (testing the hypothesis). Next, the results are checked (data analysis). Finally, the results are acted upon (rethinking the hypothesis).[9] And so, once the change has been made, its effectiveness is documented, with the aim to decrease variation within the entire system, thus making the community a healthier place in which to live. While this formal approach to problem solving provides an excellent structure to create positive changes and growth, the initial attempts at applying CQI to the perinatal project were much less formalized. Instead, a few individuals concentrated on the philosophy behind the new approach and used those theories as a guide with the hope that this type of problem solving could help the status of healthcare.

Within this structure, Miles felt that an initial step to improve perinatal morbidity and mortality was to look upstream and concentrate on prenatal care itself, and so his hypothesis—that women who do not receive prenatal care are more likely to have high-risk infants—was tested. This statement is based on the fact that prenatal care is associated with improved perinatal morbidity, but it is unclear what aspects of prenatal care account for this association.[10] By focusing on the area of prenatal care, those involved in the project hoped to see a decrease in neonatal intensive care admissions, a decrease in long-term morbidity of children, and an increase in the overall health of the community. The team that was organized to approach this problem was not an official quality improvement team of the hospital, and its members changed as new areas were addressed. Miles initiated and led many of the efforts of the group and was aided by Bingham of MVRMC, Cheryl Juntensen, director of Public Health District V, Maggi Machala, pregnancy program coordinator for Public Health District V, and the ob-gyn physicians in Twin Falls. The group was organized to meet as a whole in making major decisions, but otherwise individuals would carry out their own projects.

In an attempt to clarify the process of prenatal care current at the time, the group tried to use the perspective of the consumer—the patient—to see how the process worked from that viewpoint. Flowcharts were used in attempting to identify obstacles to care. An informal analysis of access to prenatal care was performed by Machala, and a questionnaire was given to mothers who had delivered at MVRMC in an attempt to identify any complaints and concerns they had about their care. Once all of this information was gathered, the group was able to name some areas for improvement. These areas included educating the patient about the hospital before she arrived in labor, improving time delays once in the hospital, and ensuring prenatal care to avoid drop-in deliveries. Within the community, improvement areas focused on access, efficiency, and affordability of care. It was clear to Miles that any efforts at improving the current process could greatly benefit the patient population, but the process of this improvement could be time-consuming and difficult.

As a means of reducing the variation of care within the system, the group tried to identify the main problem areas (Illustration 3.2). With respect to access to prenatal care, multiple factors from financial to psychosocial were impeding the process. In 1988, Medicaid eligibility was set at 43 percent of the federal poverty level, which gave insurance to a small number of people in need. However, even for those who were fortunate enough to receive Medicaid, the reimbursement for prenatal care and delivery was only $400, an amount that did not cover the physician's overhead. Also, from the delivering physician's point of view, many of these patients who could not afford their care were also high-liability concerns with multiple, time-consuming psychosocial issues. The availability of physicians was also a problem. In the area were five obstetricians, located in Twin Falls, with all other deliveries performed by family practitioners. However, if a family practitioner performed more than 40 deliveries per year, then his or her malpractice insurance greatly increased.[11] And so, in an area lacking adequate numbers of physicians, not all patients could receive care, and those cut out of the system were the ones who could not pay or were difficult to manage.

Illustration 3.2   Obstacles to Prenatal Care

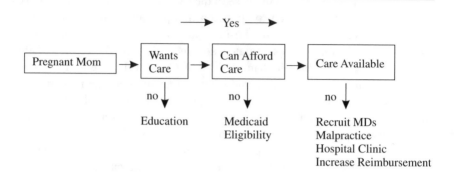

With respect to the efficiency of the system, the obstacles to improvement were identified by Machala.[11] She revealed the difficulty that patients were experiencing because of having to make multiple visits to multiple care sites with numerous delays. A patient making different visits to different sites, for pregnancy testing as well as for Women, Infants, and Children (WIC) and Medicaid reimbursement, would increase the physician-to-patient ratio. Also, the group saw the need to improve the efficiency of clinic visits for the public health patient population. And last, they saw patient education as a necessary component of improving the patient's and community's health while preventing future problems.

Instituting these improvement goals was a long process, and at times different members of the group led the effort. In an attempt to increase the affordability of care by increasing Medicaid eligibility, a group effort was made at the state level to lobby for change. In January 1989, the Medicaid eligibility increased from 43 percent to 67 percent of federal poverty level. Then, in August 1989,[11] the federal Office of Budget Reconciliation Act increased eligibility to 75 percent, and later, in April 1990, the level increased to 133 percent of poverty level. These efforts allowed for many more patients to have insurance and seek care.

However, this increase in Medicaid eligibility did not affect physician reimbursement or physicians' desire to take on new patients. So an eight-member committee, supported by the Idaho Medical Association and the Maternal and Child Health Committee, consisting of obstetricians, family practitioners, and pediatricians, lobbied for a change in the reimbursement policy. By 1990, a change was made that decreased pediatric hospital reimbursement to allow for an increase in obstetrical reimbursement. This effort resulted in an increase of prenatal care and delivery reimbursement from $400 to $1,200.[12]

In the area of improving access to care, MVRMC, the Public Health Department, Family Health Services (a community health clinic), and the obstetricians worked together to ensure availability and efficiency of services. At first, the health department created four decentralized area sites and incorporated "one-stop shopping" at each of these sites.[11] The health department also received a federal Maternal and Child Health grant for all women with income below the 185 percent of poverty level. This block grant ensured comprehensive and efficient prenatal care, including one-stop shopping for pregnancy testing and education, smoking cessation, applying for WIC, Medicaid screening and receipt of a temporary card, nutrition counseling, and social work intervention. This program expanded services to many women previously uninsured, and enabled the patient to be seen promptly by her physician. Timely obstetrical care could now be provided without the physician being concerned with payment or multiple psychosocial issues. Magic Valley Regional Medical Center also established an obstetrical clinic, staffed by the obstetricians in the community, to ensure that any woman wanting care could receive it if she was not able to be seen at a private office.

Another factor of access to care, the low physician-to-patient ratio, has been a problem well known to the people of Idaho, and any previous effort to improve this condition was encouraged again. However, the group was not successful with recruiting efforts, and some of the obstetricians were not willing to make recruitment a priority, concentrating instead on the other improvement areas. However, the family practitioners, who were limited because of malpractice quotas, were soon able to see more patients because the additional malpractice insurance was being paid for by the county hospitals.[11]

In an attempt to improve the patients' education and perceived need for prenatal care, the Public Health Department, through the block grant, began classes, "Baby Your Baby," to educate future mothers about pregnancy, birthing, child rearing, and contraception. The department identified the women who were smoking and tagged their charts so that all healthcare workers could encourage the patients to stop smoking. These women were also enrolled in smoking cessation classes. The health department worked to ensure that all of their patients were thus educated and informed about their healthcare.

From 1988 to 1991 all of these changes were being instituted in an attempt to test the program's hypothesis, and by the end of 1991 the group was ready to begin data analysis and to see if the expected outcome was accurate. The results would help them answer the questions: "How do we know that pregnant women are getting the best prenatal care that they can, and how do we know that the care we give works?"

With respect to affordability, the number of Medicaid deliveries increased dramatically from 123 in 1988 to 231 in 1990, the year reimbursement fees increased to $1,200 and Medicaid eligibility increased to 133 percent of the poverty level. At the same time, the number of drop-in deliveries, those women receiving no prenatal care, declined (Illustration 3.3).

The group also looked at NICU admissions as another indicator of perinatal morbidity, and again they saw a dramatic decline from 184 admissions in 1988 to 137 admissions in 1991. During this decrease in admissions the total number of deliveries at the hospital had increased. The number of NICU patient days, which gives a better indication of how sick the admissions are, showed a steady decline from 1,726 days in 1988 to 974 days in 1990. However, in 1991, the figure increased to 1,162 days. Along with this indicator, low-birthweight figures were analyzed. As hoped for, the incidence of low birth weight decreased along with the increase in prenatal care, but then increased in 1991 (Illustration 3.4).

With respect to patient education, results were not available for review. The Baby Your Baby classes were well attended, but it was difficult to assess the direct effectiveness of these sessions. Similarly, the results of the smoking cessation program are still being studied and follow-up data are being accumulated.

Financially, both increases and decreases occurred in healthcare costs. Because of the expanded eligibility rules, the number of women receiving Medicaid increased. Approximately 200 more women were enrolled, each costing an average of $2,000 per pregnancy. This increase created an additional cost of $400,000. However, along with this increased expenditure for prenatal

Illustration 3.3   Number of Drop-In Deliveries

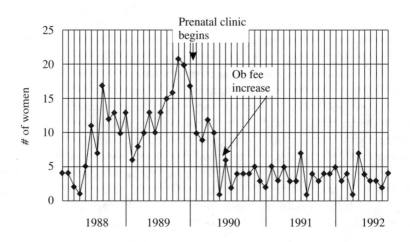

Illustration 3.4   Number of Low-Birthweight Infants

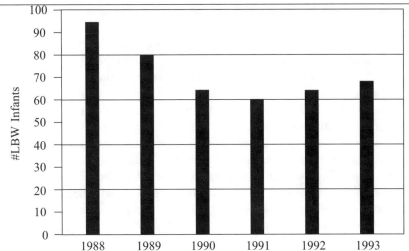

care came a decrease in NICU patient days. One day in the NICU costs an average of $1,000. In 1988, the total was 1,726 patient days, while in 1990, it decreased to 974 patient days. This change created a savings of $750,000. During 1991, when the total number of days increased to 1,162 days, the savings as compared to 1988 was still $564,000.[12]

Having found these results, the group concluded that their efforts not only had increased the number of pregnant women receiving care but also had improved the health status of their babies, directly contributing to the overall health of the community. The general agreement was to continue the current care they developed, but from their data they were able to identify some problem areas that still needed improvement. One of these areas was the increase in NICU patient days for 1991. Miles was uncertain whether this figure was part of normal variation or something that could be improved. In attempting to explain the NICU data, he discovered that the twinning rate in Twin Falls for that year had increased compared to past years. Twins are at a 50 percent higher risk for low birth weight and at a five times higher risk for mortality than are single births.[10] Miles discovered that in 1991 the twinning rate in the area was double the national average.[8] This increase was most likely the major cause for the increase in NICU patient days.

However, that odd variation of the twinning rate did not satisfy the group. Some members looked at the issue of prenatal care—its definition and implementation. Different aspects of care vary from physician to physician and, interestingly, since 1988 the rate of women beginning prenatal care within the first trimester has been steady at 60–63 percent.[1] The significance of this finding is unclear, but the group is curious to see if increasing that percentage could influence perinatal morbidity and mortality.

These areas, along with programs to improve data collection and to make better use of statistics, are some of the projects that are being considered for the group's next improvement undertaking. However, members are also aware of some inevitable roadblocks. One of the other community obstetricians has increased his prenatal care fees to $2,000, which is above the current Medicaid reimbursement amount of $1,200. It is feared that others might follow his move, possibly leading to a significant decrease in affordability and access to care. Also, five family practitioners in Twin Falls are going to stop their obstetrics service. And the hospital clinic closed with the verbal agreement that the obstetricians in town would care for anyone who needed prenatal care—but that outcome has been difficult to track. The Maternal and Child Health Block grant was discontinued in January 1992, leaving many women without access to comprehensive care, and there still remains for all patients a one-month waiting period for the first obstetrical visit. Further, the Hispanic population in the area is growing, but there are no translation services available within the healthcare system. Finally, Medicaid has stated that it will stop all payment from April 1993 to the beginning of its next fiscal year, July 1, 1993. The obstetricians and family practitioners are unsure if they will take on new patients who will be delivering and not paying for their care during the months from April to July 1993.

Miles is concerned about the course that prenatal care could take, and would like to readdress the issues of providers, access, and payment as soon as possible. He would also like to have a better understanding of what specific factors in prenatal care truly affect outcome. He has applied for a grant to develop an interactive video to educate future mothers and to develop a systems approach to prenatal care by creating a uniform database and vision within the entire region.[12] However, the views of the group are varied. Juntensen and Machala, in agreement but aware of their decreased funding, continue to follow the health department's pregnancy program annual plan that highlights the community need for prenatal care as well as the strategies to follow in continuing to improve early access and comprehensive care.[13] But because of the anticipated problems for the future of prenatal care, Machala has distributed a pregnancy program progress report (1989–1991) that emphasizes the need to increase the number of women receiving care in the first trimester. There is also concern about the appropriateness of the current content and amount of patient education and whether or not a need exists for specific education before women actually become pregnant. Mr. Bingham continues to support the efforts of the group and the mission of the hospital, but he has become aware that with this initial improvement in the health of the community, the NICU appears to be becoming underused, overstaffed, and less profitable.[7] This financial reality, while not changing Bingham's vision to improve the health of the community, is a factor that is requiring some of his attention. The obstetricians are not interested in recruiting more physicians; they want to see if there is a problem first before making any further efforts to improve prenatal care. The group plans to meet next month to decide what to do next.

Miles has asked Blackwell to plan the agenda for the next meeting and to give him her priority list for the next steps to take. Blackwell knows that Miles expects three questions to be answered: Why do we do what we do, how do we know what we do works, and how can we make what we do better?

Notes

1. Idaho Department of Health and Welfare, *Annual Summary of Vital Statistics* (Boise: IDHW, 1988, 1989, 1990).
2. Conversation with Jodi Craig, August 1992.
3. Magic Valley Regional Medical Center. *MVRMC Current State* (Twin Falls, ID, 1989).
4. M. Walton, *The Deming Management Method* (New York: Putnam Publishing Group, 1986).
5. J. Bronowski, *Science and Human Values* (New York: Harper and Row, Publishers, Inc., 1965).
6. P. M. Senge, *The Fifth Discipline* (New York: Doubleday/Currency, 1990).
7. Conversation with John Bingham, July 1992.
8. Perinatal Data Bank (Magic Valley Regional Medical Center, Twin Falls, ID, 1988).
9. Joint Commission on Accreditation of Healthcare Organizations. *Striving Toward Improvement: Six Hospitals in Search of Quality* (Oakbrook Terrace, IL, 1992).
10. N. F. Hacker and M. Moore, *Essentials of Obstetrics and Gynecology* (Philadelphia, PA: W. B. Saunders Company, 1986).
11. M. Machala and M. Miner, "Piecing Together the Crazy Quilt of Prenatal Care." *Public Health Reports* 106 (July–August 1991): 53–60.
12. P. Miles, *A Systems Approach to Rural Prenatal Care*, Unpublished grant proposal.
13. Idaho Department of Health and Welfare, *Pregnancy Program Annual Plan* (Boise: IDHW, 1992).

Quality Cost Report: Klee Hospital

Gina Restieri

Klee Hospital is a 600-bed facility located in a large city. The hospital was built in 1920. A new wing housing approximately 100 beds was built in 1960, and minor renovations and upkeep have occurred internally, but the basic structure of the hospital remains as it was built in 1920.

The hospital has 15 medical-surgical units. Each unit has approximately 30 beds. The units are antiquated with few private rooms. Most of the rooms are semiprivate with between two and four patients per room. Few units have bathrooms in the room; most have community bathrooms and showers. The current Hospital Information System (HIS) was installed in 1980 to allow for easy access to laboratory results. The computer terminals are located at each nursing station, pharmacy, and laboratory.

Over the past five years, Klee Hospital has experienced serious economic hardships as a result of the changing healthcare marketplace. The increasing role of managed care organizations and changes in reimbursement systems are a major cause of the recent losses the hospital has experienced. In addition, Klee Hospital, once a premier hospital catering to the wealthy patients of the area, has now experienced an influx of immigrants, most of whom either do not have insurance or are Medicare/Medicaid recipients. As a result of these changes, administrators have been forced to downsize staff positions and to close hospital units, leaving 500 operational beds.

The Board of Directors knows changes in management are necessary. The remaining staff are disgruntled with the hospital, contend that patient care is being compromised, and are fearful that they, too, will lose their jobs. Many of the staff have been with the hospital for 20 to 30 years and are angry. In the beginning of the year, the Board of Directors hired a new chief operating officer (COO) named Sarah Wright. The COO came to Klee Hospital with over 20 years administrative experience, excellent credentials, and an outstanding reputation for her success in modernization. Prior to taking the position at Klee Hospital, Sarah Wright worked for 18 years at a small hospital on the outskirts of the city. Some say her "go-get-'em" attitude transformed an almost defunct hospital into a technologically advanced regional hospital center. The Board of Directors at Klee Hospital hopes that Sarah Wright will bring the same successes to their hospital.

The Incident

On May 1, a 75-year-old man was admitted to a medical-surgical floor with a wound infection. The admitting nurse asked Mr. D. if he had any allergies. Mr. D. replied that he thought he might be allergic to penicillin. A moment later, the nurse was called out of the room for an emergency. A different nurse returned to the room to finish admitting the patient. She failed to indicate on the chart that the patient might have an allergy to penicillin. Later that same day a young intern, Dr. S., interviewed the patient. He also asked the patient if he had any allergies. The patient replied he was not sure if he had any allergies. The physician indicated in his notes that the patient did not have any allergies. The physician wrote an order for 1.2 million units of penicillin intravenously every six hours. The order was sent to the pharmacy. The night nurse administered the medication. The patient had an anaphylactic reaction[1] and went into respiratory arrest. The patient was then administered counteracting medications by the physician, intubated, placed on a ventilator, and transferred to the Intensive Care Unit. Mr. D. was a Medicare recipient. Under the Medicare system, the hospital was reimbursed based on the patient's DRG. The costs associated with the medication error were not reimbursed, and Klee Hospital covered these extra costs. The medication error unnecessarily cost the hospital money and caused needless hardships for the patient. Pamela Smith, director of nursing, is outraged by the incident.

Pamela Smith has been with Klee Hospital for 30 years. She started as a staff nurse and worked her way up to director of nursing. She believes the incident resulted from all of those cuts over the past five years, and has been afraid that something like this would have to happen before anyone took notice. Additionally, she has noticed an increase in the number of medication errors occurring each year. In fact, upon investigating medication errors further, she realizes that the increase in the last four years has been over 30 percent. This increase is much more than the standard 10 to 15 percent increase she was expecting to find. Smith has formed a task force, made up of nurses, doctors, pharmacists, administrators, and finance department representatives, to look into the issue. Their job is to investigate the problems of medication administration, including the costs to the hospital, and to develop possible solutions. A Quality Cost Report has been developed (Illustration 4.1) in an attempt to measure the medication administration services the hospital currently provided and could provide in the future.

Existing Hospital Policy

Klee Hospital reviews medication administration policy and procedure during the initial orientation period for new hires and distributes self-learning modules (SLM) annually for nurses, pharmacists, and physicians. The SLMs are

Illustration 4.1   Current Program at Klee Hospital

QUALITY COST REPORT

Prevention Costs
Initial Orientation	$ 23,000	Prevention costs examine the costs
Training	17,110	associated with preventing an unfavorable
Total	**$ 194,210**	incident from occurring.

Appraisal Costs
Inspections	$ 163,600	Appraisal costs represent the money
Incidence Reporting	2,000	spent to uncover failures in the
Total	**$ 165,600**	existing system.

Internal Failure Costs
Medical Related Problems	$1,192,449‡	Internal failure costs represent money
Downtime*	69,260	lost due to system design failure within
Total	**$1,261,660**	the organization.

External Failure Costs
Discharge Delay (MRP)	$ 300,000‡	External failure costs represent money
Poor Reputation†	1,000,000	lost due to system design failure outside
Total	**$1,300,000**	the organization.

Total   **$2,921,470**

* Assumption: Allotted two hours of downtime per eight-hour shift.

†Assumption: $1 million is allotted for the cost of poor reputation. The Quality Cost Report must account for the effects of poor reputation, but poor reputation is difficult to measure. $1 million is assumed to be the starting cost, and this cost will decline as prevention costs increase.

‡Schneider et al. 1995. These two numbers combined represent the cost of medical related problems (MRP) as discussed in the text.

distributed in the beginning of each year, and all staff members are expected to read the SLM on their own time.

Four "inspectors" are based in the hospital at a cost of approximately $163,600 (see Illustration 4.1). The "inspectors" review patient charts to monitor for medication errors as well as other inconsistencies. In addition, nurse managers on the units also routinely review charts for medication errors. Once an error is found, an occurrence report is completed as mandated by the state. Some disciplinary action may be taken depending on the severity of the error and the frequency of mistakes made by the same staff member.

The Task Force

The task force has concluded that approximately 100 medication errors occurred in the last year, leading to almost 2,000 incidences of additional lab work, procedures, increased length of stay, transfers to an ICU, and similar resource-consumptive activities. These medical related problems (MRP) cost the hospital approximately $1.5 million.[2] Schneider et al. had conducted a retrospective chart review from 1992–1994 of patients at a university-affiliated hospital who were known to have had adverse reactions from medical errors. The study had examined all interventions resulting directly from a medication error. According to Schneider et al., 109 patient charts were reviewed, and 1,911 MRPs were reported at estimated costs of their own medication errors. Using a similar approach, Klee Hospital has estimated the costs of their own medication errors.

The task force needs to find out what the problems are with medication administration, and what the hospital is going to be accountable for. When the wrong medication is given to the patient or when a patient is given a medication he/she is allergic to, it is clear that a medication error has occurred. But, is it a medication error when a medication is given at 2 p.m. instead of at 11 a.m.? What if a medication is given that interacts with another medication the patient was taking? What if a reaction occurs two or three weeks after the patient has left the hospital? Yes, these are all medication errors, but which medication errors is the hospital going to be concerned about and responsible for? Is Klee's problem with medication administration procedure systemwide or is it an individual problem for staff members?

The task force decides at this point that all medication errors need to be investigated. There are many apparent reasons for the increase in medication errors. Some reasons include lack of knowledge about the medication or of information about the patient, transcription errors, faulty identification of drugs, and preparation errors.[3] Although the task force wants to eliminate all medication errors, they agree that they need to concentrate on those errors that have resulted in adverse effects and have cost money. Changes in staff education, behavior, and system functioning are needed.

Solutions

At the task force meeting, Pamela Smith, director of nursing, suggested reviewing the current SLM and requiring documented proof of completion. John Douglas, M.D. recommended having two nurses check the order before medications were given. Carl Hess, M.D. suggested having patients sign a specific form indicating their allergies and health status. Sally Pane, R.N. had an idea to place a red sticker on the patient's ID band when a possible allergy was detected and suggested hiring more experienced personnel. Sarah Wright, COO recommended modernizing the medication administration system and instituting a computer system hospitalwide to eliminate illegible orders, identify errors, and expedite the overall delivery of services to the patients.

Sarah Wright listens carefully to these ideas and many others circulating at the meeting. She decides to recommend short-term and long-term goals to Samuel Sand, hospital CEO.

Short-Term Goals

1. An immediate review of the SLM contents;
2. A required post-test for SLM to be graded by an instructor and recorded with a required passing grade of 80 percent or higher;
3. An immediate distribution of review material to the hospital staff;
4. The labeling of charts and patient ID bands when an allergy was identified and mandated for the purpose not only of increasing awareness for the nurses and doctors, but also to highlight information for the chart reviewers.

Long-Term Goals

1. Development of a computer system to include the ability to order a medication and have it sent immediately to the pharmacy;
2. On-line identification of contraindications and allergies.

Wright adds that these interventions had been implemented at her former hospital and worked well.

With the approval of Samuel Sand, CEO, Sarah Wright implements the short-term goals. A memo is sent to all managers, administrators, departments, and nursing units. Wright believes these changes will work. She is convinced that preventing the medications problem from occurring will help the hospital. This type of approach worked in her former institution; it will work here.

Ron Bart is shocked by the implementation of the changes. He is angry because he disagrees with some of the costs associated with the Quality Cost Report and believes that further investigation is needed before changes are made. He believes the costs have been underestimated. The COO responds with an itemized list detailing how each cost was determined. She also reiterates that some allowance needs to be made for estimates on the cost of some quality issues that are extremely difficult to quantify.

The director of finance, Mark Fin, believes that Klee Hospital does not have the front-end monies to make any changes or develop any new programs. Sarah Wright responds to this argument by stating that the short-term changes will cost very little to implement and are really just a revision of policy and procedure. Implementing the long-term goal will be costly, but a computer system not only will decrease medication errors resulting from illegible orders and careless mistakes, but will also expedite other services and improve documentation. Adding to the cost of prevention will help to decrease hospital losses when failures occur. Some ways to finance the computer system are through fund-raising, grants, and borrowing.

Bob Burns suggests not making any changes at this time because the hospital is already in debt. Sarah Wright responds to this statement by demonstrating through the Quality Cost Report that errors are costing the hospital unnecessary amounts and that some interventions need to be made. Preventing the problem will ultimately help the hospital to save money.

A second Quality Cost Report developed one year later measures the effectiveness of the changes (see Illustration 4.2). The second Quality Cost Report demonstrates an increase in the costs of prevention and a decrease in the costs of internal and external failures. The short-term interventions have resulted in a 15 percent decline in the adverse effects of medication errors.

Based on these results, Sarah Wright approachs the CEO of the hospital with the idea of swiftly implementing the computer system in order to improve the entire system, boost hospital morale, and move the hospital into the modern era. She secures a substantial loan and private backing to cover the initial costs. The two decide to move ahead with implementation of a new computer system.

Some managers believe that the decision to install a computer system is rash, and they are angry because they were not consulted first. Pamela Smith, director of nursing, believes the hospital is functioning just fine without a computer system. Many of her nurses believe that new computers will just make their job more difficult. Mark Fin, the director of finance, is shocked that he was not consulted prior to the announcement of the new system. He

Illustration 4.2 Program with Implementation of Short-Term Goals: (1) Review of SLM; (2) Post-Test Evaluation; and (3) Chart/ID Band Labeling

QUALITY COST REPORT

Prevention Costs
Initial Orientation	$ 23,000	
Review of SLM	11,200	
Post-Test Evaluation	10,510	
Chart/ID Band Labeling	6,250	
Training/Reimplementing SLM	171,210	
Total	**$ 222,170**	

Appraisal Costs
Inspections	$ 163,600	
Incidence Reporting	1,700	15% Drop*
Total	**$ 165,300**	

Internal Failure Costs
Medical Related Problems	$1,013,540	15% Drop*
Downtime	69,260	
Total	**$1,082,800**	

External Failure Costs
Discharge Delay (MRP)	$ 255,000	15% Drop*
Poor Reputation	850,000	15% Drop*
Total	**$1,105,000**	
Total	**$2,575,270**	

* Assumption: The implementation of the short-term goals will bring a 15 percent drop in failures that occur subsequent to medication errors.

believes Sarah Wright is only interested in modernization and is not concerned about what is best for the hospital, the staff, and the patients.

A third Quality Cost Report is developed the following year to show the costs associated with installation of the new Hospital Information System (Illustration 4.3). The third Quality Cost Report further demonstrates how increasing prevention has helped to decrease economic losses associated with errors and other failures. An additional 20 percent decline in medical related problems has resulted from the implementation of a computer system.

Medication errors are at the lowest level in the last ten years. The Board of Directors is delighted with the accomplishments of Sarah Wright and felt strongly that they have made the right choice in bringing her to Klee Hospital. However, staff turnover is at its highest. Many positions are going unfilled. Staff

Illustration 4.3   After Implementation of Long-Term Goals: (1) Computer
System; (2) Database of Allergies/Contraindications

QUALITY COST REPORT

Prevention Costs

Initial Orientation Costs	$ 23,000	
Review of SLM	11,200	
Post-Test Evaluation	10,510	
Chart/ID Band Labeling	6,250	
Training/Reimplementing SLM	171,210	
Computer System (depreciated)	800,000	Long-Term Goal*
Total	**$1,022,170**	

Appraisal Costs

Inspections	$ 163,600	
Incidence Reporting	1,360	20% Drop†
Operation and Maintenance	1,000,000	
Total	**$1,164,960**	

Internal Failure Costs

Medical Related Problems	$ 810,832	20% Drop†
Downtime	69,260	
Total	**$ 880,092**	

External Failure Costs

Discharge Delay (MRP)	$ 204,000	20% Drop†
Poor Reputation	680,000	20% Drop†
Total	**$ 884,000**	
Total	**$3,951,222**	

* Cost of computer system spread over ten years. Total cost is $8,000,000.

† Assumption: The computer system will bring a 20 percent drop in failures that occur subsequent to medication errors.

members dislike their additional responsibilities and feel that the computer
system only requires extra time.

Notes

1. A severe allergic reaction usually occurs immediately after the administering of a
   drug. B. Kozier and G. Erb, *Fundamentals of Nursing* (Boston: Addison-Wesley
   Publishing Co., 1987).
2. P. Schneider et al. "Cost of Medication-related Problems at a University Hospital."
   American Journal of Health System Pharmacists 52 (1995): 2415–18.
3. Lucian Leape et al., "Systems Analysis of Adverse Drug Events." *Journal of the
   American Medical Association* 274 (5 July 1995): 37.

Physician Specialists in Inpatient Care?

Mark Stein and Anthony R. Kovner

To: Physician Executive Group

From: Mark Conerly, M.D.
Medical Director

Date: March 1996

Re: Inpatient Physician Specialist

I would like to discuss the topic of an inpatient physician. The rationale for having a physician dedicated to the care of hospitalized patients is that length of stay can be reduced while quality of care is improved. The concept is akin to that of specialization, such as nephrology or cardiology, and in this case, hospitalization. This concept has already caught on in California and in the Southwest and is being tried in various centers in Massachusetts and Washington, D.C. Most of the centers that I am familiar with employ a combination of pulmonologists/intensivists and cardiologists since these two organ systems seem to be the discharge rate limiting steps and represent problems requiring the most active and intense treatment.

If the medical group is only to do a pilot project, then there would be a limited number of patients in the hospital at any given time for the in-hospital physician to care for. Therefore, we would at most need one such physician and, in most likelihood, one-half of a physician.

1. Should we subcontract a physician from the full-time department of medicine? These doctors are available and well-trained, but are difficult to incentivize and are part of a fairly rigid bureaucracy.

2. Should this physician be an existing medical group doctor? Some of them are willing to participate but have little experience or training in this role.

3. Should we hire or subcontract one of the intensivists currently working at the hospital? They are the best-trained and experienced physicians, but they also have the longest length of stay and highest utilization.

4. Should we hire an outside intensivist who is interested and well-versed with this role? This may be the most expensive option and would pose difficulty with coverage.

The next issue concerns our own physicians. We would like the option of an in-hospital physician to be purely voluntary. Some of our physicians have already expressed an interest in not caring for hospitalized patients and in giving up this role to a "specialist." The problem here is that if we make this choice optional, we may never develop a critical mass of patients to sustain a full-time in-hospital physician.

There is no easy answer to this situation, not to mention questions of integration into an on-call and coverage schedule, integration of the in-house physician with the emergency department, and compensation. This is why we have not implemented a pilot study already. I am hopeful that we can make some progress during our meeting.

The Meeting

The physician executive group was made up of the following members: Sam Tittle, hospital medical director; Willie Brown, associate dean of the medical school; Clark Simms, associate director of pediatrics; and Bernie Hostetler, affiliated group medical director. A summary of highlights of their discussion follows:

Tittle: This hospital is becoming an intensive care unit. Fee-for-service is rewarding many consultations being done for internists who aren't specialists in hospital medicine. This is an extremely expensive practice.

Conerly: What we want to do in the group is reduce costs for the medical group; also, we have doctors who practice far away but who want to be affiliated with an academic health center. Our purpose is to decrease cost and improve outcomes. Secondarily, we want to increase referrals from unaffiliated physicians into the medical center.

Brown: Why don't you form groups of four internists, one of whom becomes an inpatient specialist? They can rotate the hospital work among themselves and stay current in both fields.

Simms: Your doctors aren't working enough hours. After working 35 or 40 hours a week in office practice, they should visit their hospital patients before or after office hours.

Hostetler: Won't continuity of care be a problem with inpatient specialists? How broadly based do you want the inpatient specialist to be? And what happens over time to the office-based physician whose knowledge base and clinical skills erode? What happens to the ability to recruit physicians downstream? They may not be marketable elsewhere after practicing and not visiting their patients in the hospital.

Brown: Conceding that there are best practice physicians for certain diagnoses, why not mandate consultants for that diagnosis and let an existing hospital specialist be "co-pilot" for that patient? From the point of view of the medical school, I would be very hesitant to accredit one-dimensional physicians, such as you suggest.

Simms: In pediatrics, the inpatient hospital specialist works very well because there are fewer inpatients per pediatrician. And the pediatricians stay in touch with their patients and families even if the inpatient specialist is in charge. Your physicians can do the same with their adult patients.

Conerly: It's not easy to teach physicians to use protocols. There's also the issue of accessing test results more quickly than we do and getting the patients out earlier. There's no question that the inpatient specialists get the patients out earlier, the patients don't complain, and my internists don't want to spend two months every year in the hospital on teaching rounds. This accounts for a 15 percent loss in productivity.

Tittle: What we want is to be "branding" our 25 satellite center docs to the medical center to attract patients for managed care contracts and others. We can't have a real disconnect between these docs and the medical center.

Conerly: I came into this meeting wanting to implement inpatient hospital specialists, which I see being of advantage to the medical center, not merely for the group, but now I'm not so sure.

Short Case C

CQI at Suburban Hospital

Larry K. McReynolds

Clara Maass Health System is composed of a 475-bed community hospital, 120-bed long-term facility, 10-bed subacute unit, and visiting nurse agency located in north Newark, New Jersey. The hospital is the largest entity of the health system, having been in existence for 125 years. As a community-based nonteaching hospital, the medical staff is an older, conservative group weary of change. The employees pride themselves on being part of their local hospital but have recently become disturbed at the changes occurring in their health system.

The introduction of managed care into the local marketplace has caused the hospital administration much worry that change must occur to service in the immediate future. Here are some of the key factors causing concern right now:

1. The county in which Clara Maass is located has 14 other hospitals, making the county overbedded by 200 percent.

2. The competitive environment is enabling managed care companies to force hospitals to take rates below their costs.

3. The hospital's average length of stay and average cost per discharge are significantly higher than those of other hospitals in the area.

4. Many of the physicians are close to retirement and see little cause to change their ways of practicing medicine at this stage of the game.

5. Employee morale is low due to cost-cutting, two recent layoffs, and having received no raise for two years.

Implementation of a CQI program by administration is an attempt to help bring about some of the needed changes in the organization. The hospital CQI program has been approved by the board of trustees and has been in place for almost two years.

Implementation of the CQI program was accomplished through required CQI training for managers, all employees, and as many physicians as possible. Initially, quality action teams (QAT) were chartered to examine clinical and operational issues. The patient services department selected the CareMap format for addressing physician and multidisciplinary issues. CareMaps are multidisciplinary tools for establishing protocols, outcomes, and length of stay.

CareMaps were developed using the primary nurse model placing the nurse as the responsible party for keeping the patient on the map. Operational QATs were chartered by the steering committee to address processes and procedures that were high-volume, problem prone, costly, or likely to have an adverse effect on the patient. Elements predictive of patient satisfaction were also used to determine if a quality action team should be chartered.

To facilitate integration of CQI principles among all employees, managers attend an ongoing workshop. This monthly meeting is designed to provide a nonthreatening forum for managers to examine their department processes and outcomes and the degree of the department's success in meeting the customer's needs. Ideas from the workshop and suggestions from the CareMap and QATs are approved by the steering committee and implemented by the team.

Case Questions

- Employees have the feeling that eliminating "wasted work" and improving processes is a fancy way of eliminating more jobs. Identify strategies to overcome this impression.
- Managers feel this is the management philosophy of the meek. Identify and describe effective means to overcome this barrier.
- Physicians see CareMaps as cookbook medicine imposed upon them by the nursing department. Describe ways to obtain their buy-in into CareMaps.
- Identify organizational strategies that the hospital should adopt to make the institution more viable in the marketplace.

Short Case D

ER at Queens Hospital Center

Anthony R. Kovner

Now 83 percent of patients are treated and released. They wait six to eight hours for treatment. The goal is to decrease waiting time and the number of walkouts and to improve care and patient satisfaction.

Current Procedure:

Step 1. Patient seen by triage nurse.

Step 2. Patient sent to registration.

Step 3. Patient waits to be seen by physician.

Step 4. Patient sent for any necessary lab or x-ray.

Step 5. Patient waits for test results to be reviewed by MD.

Step 6. Patient treated, discharged, or admitted.

Case Question

- What do you suggest to improve the process? To reduce errors by the triage nurse?

Short Case E

Sparks Medical Center and the Board of Trustees

Anthony R. Kovner

Sam Phillips, chairman of Sparks Medical Center's board of trustees wondered why hospital board meetings were so different from those at Phillips' Flavors, Inc. The hospital board discussed the reports of various committees, reviewed accreditation and licensing reports, and listened to reports and recommendations about state regulations and reimbursement. At Phillips' Flavors, Inc., the board discussed the future of business, what the competition was doing, and strategies to increase market share and profit margins.

Clara Burns, CEO of Sparks Medical Center, made the following recommendations to Sam Phillips regarding more effective board meetings:

1. Board discussion should focus on the organization's mission.

2. Objectives and strategies should be established.

3. A work plan to plan and measure board performance should be developed.

Sam realized that the problem with addressing these issues was the board structure and organization and the amount of time taken up at meetings by routine committee and management reports. This resulted in a full agenda and little time to deal with issues critical to the future of the Medical Center.

Case Questions

- What do you recommend that Sam do now?
- Identify constraints and opportunities that Sam faces in implementing your recommendations.

Part **III**

Organization Design

Introduction

In healthcare, discussion about organizational design occurs at four levels. The first is at the patient care level under capitation and managed care. New questions are being asked. How do we organize the best care for asthma or hypertension or back pain? This requires a definition of "best," data on the population served, a team of staff members working to achieve these goals, and management support. How does our organization answer these questions? What is excellent diabetes care? How would we know we are achieving it?

At the next level of aggregation are the issues of the design of the hospital, nursing home, and other care organizations. How do we put the component departments together? Restructuring, re-engineering, and downsizing are the jargon terms of the moment. The Wise Medical Center case raised some of these issues, as does the VNA of Cleveland case.

Across the country, hospitals, clinics, and insurers are grouping themselves together as systems of care. In an urban area where 30 separate hospitals once stood, there may now be four competing groups of hospitals. These may be non-profit organizations, investor-owned such as Columbia HCA, or a mix of both. This is the third level of organizational design.

One reason for these changes is the recognition that with managed care we shall need many fewer hospital beds than we now have. The leaders of a single hospital left out of such a system may well wonder if they will be one of the hospitals that will disappear. One way these mergers are occurring is through the sale of a non-profit hospital to a for-profit group. The sale price plus the non-profit hospital's existing endowment is put into a non-profit foundation. The income from this foundation's endowment is used to achieve the charitable and philanthropic goals of the original non-profit hospital. The hospital, now part of the for-profit organization, will be run along business lines in a very competitive environment.

In the rush to become one of the three or four biggest groups in the area, the system bases its decisions about organizational design on expediency, comfort level, and speed rather than organizing to provide expeditious, excellent care. The local rush for size is of vital importance in a market oversupplied with hospitals. Any one urban hospital priced too high or of average quality can be ignored by a managed care system. For such a hospital to exist, it will have to accept whatever price the managed care systems choose to offer, which will not be high. If the system is large enough and includes popular, specialized, and prestigious hospitals, then all managed care systems or insurers must deal with them. Such a system will not be a "price taker," but a "price giver." It can charge a full price for its services because the HMO or insurer has no choice.

The fourth level is at the state or national policy level. The most notable effort in the last few years to change the context of healthcare delivery was the Clinton administration's unsuccessful national health plan initiative.

Currently, the devolution of decision making related to Medicaid from the federal to the state level will also change the context of care. Some states such as Hawaii and Oregon are providing interesting examples of system reform.

It is the interaction of all four of these levels of organization and system design that makes healthcare delivery a most lively arena. The field is creating unprecedented opportunities for creative leadership and the organizing of whole new ways of providing better care at lower cost.

The Cases

The coordination of many different professional workers with different skills, different views of the world, different perceptions of what needs to be done, and working under different licensing statutes lies at the heart of this new design for health services organizations.

There are many different ways of organizing work in large health services organizations: by task or purpose, by facility, or by client group served. Often, several different organizing principles operate in the same organization, sometimes appropriately and sometimes for historical reasons. As Clibbon and Sachs have pointed out, a laboratory is a place, obstetrics is a health condition, outpatients are people, dietary is a service, intensive care is a need, day care is a category of residential status, radiology is a group of techniques and rehabilitation is a purpose.[1]

The structure of many healthcare organizations was more appropriate for conditions when the organization was founded than it is today. Organization structure is determined in part by the nature of the work the organization has to do, its physical facilities, the history of the organization, and the culture of the society and of like institutions.

As academic health centers respond to competitive pressures, their organizational structures may have to be adapted for optimum organizational survival and growth. Sam Spellman has devised an ambitious reorganization plan for Wise Medical Center. What would happen if nothing is done and the current organizational structure is retained? What are the costs and benefits of Spellman's proposal? What are the problems and constraints Spellman faces in implementing his proposal? If the new methods for organizing make so much sense, why aren't other academic health centers already implementing them?

The Betterman Memorial Hospital case describes the unintended consequences of the corporate reorganization of a small rural hospital. Changing the organization structure created new, dysfunctional human relations. Once such conflicts start they are not easily reversed.

The case "Changing Role of Stakeholders in the Delivery of Healthcare" describes how one hospital is trying to respond to environmental changes with a redesign of governance and management, while being consistent with its traditional mission.

Case Questions

Proposal for the Restructuring of Wise Medical Center

- What are the arguments for and against restructuring?
- What are the preconditions necessary to allow such restructuring to take place?
- What are the key obstacles to restructuring?
- How can these obstacles be overcome?
- What do you advise Sam Spellman to do? Why?

The Corporate Reorganization of Betterman Memorial Hospital

- What do you suggest should have been done differently when corporate reorganization was first considered?
- What do you recommend for the administrator to do now?

Changing Role of Stakeholders in the Delivery of Healthcare

- Under the present structure, can the board provide clear direction for the future?
- Is the current organizational structure adequate for a managed care environment?
- Can the organization function efficiently and market itself as a unified body? (Can the organization speak as one voice?)

• Did the Northeast board clearly define its role, management's role, the medical staff's role?

• To what extent does reorganizing the governing structure guarantee success in achieving the strategic goals?

Notes

1. Sheila Clibbon and Marvin L. Sachs, "Health Care Facilities: An Alternative to Bailiwick Planning in Patient Fostering Spaces," *The New Physician* 18 (June 1969): 462–471.

Selected Bibliography

Burns, Lawton R., and Darrell P. Thorpe. "Trends and Models in Physician-Hospital Organization." *Health Care Management Review* 18, no. 4 (1993): 7–20.

Center for Health Research, Kaiser Permanente, Portland Oregon. *The State Health Insurance Program of Hawaii: From Legislative Priority to Reality.* The Center, 10 December 1991.

Griffith, John R. *The Well-Managed Health Care Organization*, 3rd Edition. Chicago: Health Administration Press, 1995, ch. 4.

Johnson, Everett A., Montague Brown, and Richard L. Johnson. *The Economic Era of Health Care: A Revolution in Organized Delivery Systems.* San Francisco: Jossey-Bass, 1996.

Johnson, Haynes, and David S. Broder. *The System: The American Way of Politics at the Breaking Point.* Boston: Little Brown, 1996.

Lathrop, J. P. "The Patient-Focused Hospital." *Healthcare Forum Journal* 34, no. 4 (1991): 16–21.

McDonagh, K. J. (ed.). *Patient-Centered Hospital Care: Reform from Within.* Chicago: Health Administration Press, 1993.

Shortell, S. M. "The Future of Hospital-Physician Relationships. Revisiting the Garden: Medicine and Management in the 1990s." *Frontiers of Health Services Management* 7, no. 1 (fall 1990): 3–32.

U.S. Congress, Office of Technology Assessment. *Evaluation of the Oregon Medical Proposal.* Publication No. OTA-H-531. Washington, DC: U.S. Government Printing Office, May 1992.

Case 6

A Proposal for the Restructuring of Wise Medical Center

Anthony R. Kovner and Louis Liebhaber

This proposal is written by Sam Spellman, Chief Operating Officer, to stimulate a discussion regarding the future structure of a 700-bed hospital in a large midwestern city. Wise Medical Center (WMC) faces the enormous challenge of delivering healthcare services in an external environment whose only hallmarks are chaos and change. Issues of an unprecedented nature confront us and will continue to do so at an increasingly rapid pace with increasingly higher stakes.

Some examples of these issues include:

- Epidemics of AIDS, TB, drug abuse, and mental illness;
- Overnight shifts in surgical techniques, such as laparoscopy, that will continue to burgeon;
- Significant shifts from inpatient to ambulatory surgery;
- Provider shifts such as a major pending penetration of managed care into the urban market;
- Tremendous momentum for a significant change in the financing of healthcare;
- Regulatory and marketplace controls to support the new financing options;
- Greater consumer involvement in treatment decisions;
- Biotechnological treatments for diseases, resulting in a variety of dislocations: medical versus surgical treatment of an increasing number of

diseases; earlier detection of some diseases; extraordinarily expensive treatment, etc.;

- Unprecedented competition among various sectors—hospitals, for-profit niche companies, outpatient options, and physicians;
- State drive for capitation of Medicaid in two years;
- Increasingly expensive—possibly rationed technology;
  —and more—

In the face of these and challenges as yet uncontemplated, the question is: *Will the Existing Organizational Structure of an Acute Care Teaching Hospital Provide Enough Agility, Adaptability, and Swiftness to Maintain or Surpass Its Current Position in the Marketplace (Financially Sound, Clinically Respected, etc.)?*

Lessons from other sectors of the economy would provide us with a resounding word of caution at complacency regarding the shape of our organization.

- Fully half of the Fortune 500 companies that were on the Fortune 500 list in 1980 were no longer on that list in 1990.
- In order to avoid sliding farther into an abyss, IBM recently split itself into 13 separate companies.
- ATT split into multiple companies and is now more successful than ever before in its history.
- GM fell asleep and lost unprecedented BILLIONS of dollars while other new entries to that heavy industry were making unprecedented profits, etc., etc.
- Major teaching hospitals in our city have lost millions of dollars in the past several years.

There are multiple lessons to be learned from what is happening in the world around us. We should examine that world and at least discuss and think through ways for us to adapt to it so that we can remain successful into the future. Below I have set out some thoughts whose origins come from many places, including thoughts and discussion which have already begun to surface at WMC. I offer the scenario below as a jumping-off point for discussion and development, not as a complete prescription for the future.

What Are the Organizational Key Concepts to WMC's Future Given the Premise of Unprecedented Continual Change?

How can an organization such as WMC anticipate change, adjust course, refocus resources, refocus our staff, and achieve equilibrium until the next change that must be anticipated and addressed?

I would argue that one response to this question is to redesign our organization into a manageable number of smaller, more autonomous business entities. These smaller entities (described in detail below) would be organized around the major current businesses of WMC. They would have a degree of autonomy that would facilitate decision making, respond to the environment, and, most importantly, foster a far greater sense of commitment and purpose to each entity. Such autonomy—with clear accountability—would foster a passionate focus while at the same time adding synergy to the whole.

The organization that would evolve would be flatter, more responsive and accountable, lower-cost, and much more agile and responsive to our various customers.

WMC would be divided into at least the following businesses. These businesses would be linked to the whole through a set of accountabilities and organizational structure and support. There must clearly be a balance, however, which recognizes that the success of the whole is more dependent on the success of the individual pieces than in the current structure.

The businesses would be:

- *The Surgical Hospital* (to include all surgical services including the ORs, endoscopy, ambulatory, surgery, etc.)
- *The Private Attending Medical Hospital* (an expansion of what we now call AOS—with the added involvement of the private attendings in the management and definition of the unit)
- *The General Medical Hospital* (the medicine and nonsurgical teaching service)
- *The Maternal and Child Health Hospital* (pediatrics and obstetrics)
- *Ambulatory Care Business* (to include clinics, managed care, and faculty practice)
- *Psychiatric and Substance Abuse Hospital*
- *Rehabilitation Institute*
- *Alternative Site Corporation* (dialysis, home care, and ???)
- *Clinical Support Entities* (radiology, lab, cardiology, etc.)

- *Corporate Services*—with potentially several sub-companies (to include food services, housekeeping, security, training, human resources, information systems, etc.)

All of the entities above were given titles that are intended to identify not only the activities and functions that are included, but also to distinguish them as major lines of business—hence, the word "division" is not used, but the word hospital is—to signify a high degree of autonomy and scope.

Each of the major entities would be led by a COO or jointly led by a high-level administrative leader or physician or both. These leaders would be charged with the integrity, bottom-line performance, quality assurance, development and carrying out of a set of strategic and long-range objectives, and each would be accountable to the central management of WMC.

Each entity would have a specific focus. Some are obviously direct providers of patient care. In that role they are charged with developing and growing their piece of the WMC business. Because the management is clearly focused and is responsible for a relatively manageable-sized entity, where all of the employees and medical staff can actually know each other and where a clear ethic, purpose, and accountability can be established, the likelihood of success in meeting the needs of customers and in anticipating and reacting to the environment should be greatly enhanced.

For example:

The Surgical Hospital

The leadership would focus on the present and future environment for surgery. What are the trends? What are the threats and opportunities? What are the needs of our current and potential customers? How do we organize, refocus, communicate, and operationalize the necessary response? Take any specific example—let's say laparoscopic surgery. The Surgical Hospital leadership would be expected to understand and anticipate the implications of laparoscopic surgical growth and change; confer with its constituents—the surgeons of various specialties; develop a business approach to the issue—which might include a plan for acquiring equipment, training skilled technical staff, regearing the ORs for the technology, and a marketing plan to HMOs for LOS reduction, and so on. The changing focus, which might also include redirecting resources on the inpatient side, could be communicated to all of the staff in the Surgical Hospital so that they could in turn prepare for and contribute to the successful implementation of the change.

The above example differs from the current environment in several important ways:

- Management of our major businesses would be focused specifically on those businesses. The success of those businesses would also be clearly focused on defined individuals with defined resources.

- The size of the entity would be such that the management can communicate effectively with all of the players: the more rapid the need to change, and the more profound the changes that might occur, the greater the need for meaningful, comprehensive buy-in and communication. That communication is infinitely more likely to succeed in an organization one can touch and feel, and also in an organization with which the players can much more closely identify.

- Each entity would be less captive to the bureaucracy and more focused on its mission and customers.

- Each entity, because of its focus and size, increases the likelihood of harnessing the potential of our CQI effort and the potential power of the human imagination and the creativity of our workforce.

- These entities are much more likely to operate with a higher degree of internal accountability and consistency. Innovation can be introduced and can take hold much more successfully.

- The new entities, as will be described below, have fewer layers in their organization structure, the result of which is lower cost, more agility, more resources focused on the end result.

- As will be described below, the entities become discerning purchasers of service rather than part of the structure that may limit the positive effects of competition and innovation.

If one looks at some of the more successful and market-sensitive (defined as agile and remaining cutting edge) entities in WMC, they are relatively self-contained units managed by a focused group of people with a well-defined mission: *Hospice, Rehab, Dialysis, Stuy Square, the Long-Term Care Division* (and even specific inpatient units such as Substance Abuse, MICU, SICU, etc.).

For an example of a functional entity as opposed to a direct business entity let's take a look at *Corporate Services:*

Corporate Services comprises those nonclinical functions that support the direct delivery of our main services (patient care). Corporate Services are functions such as billing, housekeeping, food service, security, MIS, marketing, human resources, and so forth. Under the proposed plan they would function for the most part as subcontractors to provide service to the delivery arm. As subcontractors they would be held to a standard of performance that one would expect in the competitive world of subcontracting. If the subcontractor for food service, as an example, could not demonstrate that it was providing a market-competitive product at a market-competitive price, then the service entity would have the option to subcontract that service. Even if we were ultimately constrained from actually subcontracting out the service, the specter, to the management and workers of food service, might drive innovation and improvement.

In this scheme every service, almost without exception, could be viewed as a subcontractor with the potential to be replaced by a competitor. The only service I could not envision being reasonably subjected to this provision is MIS—and that is only because of the constant state of development in which we find ourselves. It is not inconceivable that we could hire a service bureau and contract out most of MIS also. Even billing could be subjected to a "show me" scenario.

Clearly there are pitfalls to subcontracting but they may be seriously counterbalanced by the competitiveness, innovation, cost reduction, and flexibility this approach could engender. Further, if our services were so far superior, we could do as we have in food service, and the food service function could seek to provide services on a for-profit basis to other hospitals or businesses.

The raison d'etre of Corporate Services (as with the other functional support entity, Clinical Support) is to provide responsive, cost-efficient support to the main business entities of WMC. Corporate and Clinical Services would provide the services and expertise that would not necessarily be economically feasible to subdivide in each business entity, and the provision of which would simply encumber or side-track the efforts of the management of the business entity with tasks that were tangential, albeit a necessary part of their business.

The Flatter Organization

The organization described above gets flatter than the current organization in several ways.

First, each direct care delivery entity—for example, the *Private Attending Medical Hospital*—is of a manageable size (approximately 150 to 225 beds, 400 to 600 employees). All of the direct service providers and subcontractors are accountable to the COO of each entity. There would be a highly skilled nurse manager and/or head clinician and administrative type (although the latter structure may be less appealing) responsible for each patient care unit within the entity. All of the staff who worked on the unit would be directly accountable to the unit leadership (akin to the Planetree model, although this proposal goes several steps further). The unit managers (whether nurse or some combination) report directly to the COO; with only five to ten units (maximum size), this should be possible.

Second, there would be a natural imperative in this unit-based scenario to redefine some unit-based jobs—innovate to run more smoothly and cohesively—that is, possibly combining patient-focused jobs such as housekeeping, food service, and nurses aide functions.

Third, given the competitive subcontractor model described above, it will be impossible for many services to be market-competitive with the bureaucracy and layering currently in place. These layers are a part of the current fabric and cannot easily be replaced without a different sort of organization to serve.

I am not sure if it is possible to enter into this sort of organizational restructuring on a "pilot" basis, simply because it is so contrary to the current organizational structure that there is far too much potential for undermining, confusion, and waste if there are two parallel tracks.

Sam Spellman convened a meeting of top managers to discuss his proposal for restructuring WMC. These included Paul Bones, chief of medicine; Pam Ewing, vice president for nursing; Tom Starks, director of human services; Tony Rivers, vice president for finance; Lew Oakley, director of planning; and Carl Smith, the WMC CEO. A summary of highlights from their discussion follows:

Tony Rivers: Don't we have enough on our minds without drastically reorganizing patient care services? We should be focusing our energies on organizing up for managed care rather than on the internal production of services.

Paul Bones: How are we going to factor in our teaching and research objectives and strategies? We should be paying more attention to teaching and research, since this is what makes us distinctive as a hospital.

Pam Ewing: Where does nursing service figure in all this restructuring? It looks to me as if we would be losing a lot of power with no guarantee that services would be better or cheaper. You're going to put the doctors in charge of the nurses, and I'm not so sure that they ought to be telling us what to do or how we can best work together.

Tom Starks: How are you going to bring the unions into this kind of restructuring?

Lew Oakley: Are you suggesting that we could start contracting out a service like our planning department? Wouldn't there be tremendous costs in developing and evaluating different proposals plus a lot of uncertainty created among my staff, who are doing the best possible job that they know how to do?

Carl Smith: Sam, I think your scheme is a great idea, and I think the people at Hopkins and elsewhere have carried it out with some pretty impressive results. What worries me is that (1) only a few places nationally have gone into this, and the expenditures in training and planning and executive attention would be very great at a time—now—when we're under a lot of pressure to lower our costs; (2) where are WMC's champions to fight for development and implementation of this imaginative proposal? and (3) do our chiefs really have the skills and experience necessary to run these divisions? We didn't recruit them because they were excellent managers, but rather because of their leadership capabilities to run first-rate teaching programs and stimulate the production of research within their specialty.

The Corporate Reorganization of Betterman Memorial Hospital

Duncan Neuhauser

Betterman is a not-for-profit, 25-bed community general hospital in a small rural town in a predominantly rural state. Responding to the problems of rising healthcare costs, the state legislature empowered the State Insurance Commission to review and define hospital reimbursement. By 1980, Betterman Memorial Hospital was fortunate enough to have accumulated an endowment of $3 million, largely from gifts from a few wealthy families. Other hospitals in this state were not as fortunate. The State Insurance Commission proposed to deduct at least the interest from this endowment from revenues the hospital would receive from third party payors, thus making these assets worthless to Betterman Hospital. It was even rumored that some commission hotheads wanted to eliminate all reimbursement to the hospital until this endowment was entirely used up.

In order to avert these threats to the endowment, the hospital rushed through a corporate reorganization, going from a single corporation to three (see Illustration 7.1 further on).

The Corporate Structure

The *incorporators,* numbering about 250 people, live in the area and vote approval for new members. They meet once a year (about 50 incorporators attend) to hear an upbeat report on the hospital, vote for new incorporators, and endorse the slate of trustees of the foundation, proposed by the nominating committee of the foundation trustees.

The not-for-profit *foundation* holds the endowment assets, and its trustees meet monthly with the administrator and chief financial officer. In this small organization, these two administrators manage all three organizations. The hospital itself is the largest part and consumes most of their time. The foundation trustees approve board members for the two other corporations for three years at a time. These terms are renewable and appointments are staggered.

The *for-profit* subsidiary is a small undertaking that generates revenues, one-fiftieth of what the hospital does. Any profits this subsidiary makes go to the foundation. The *not-for-profit* Betterman Hospital and its board are involved in the direct management of the hospital. Its board meets monthly or more often, as needed. The administrators and chief financial officer staff and meet with all three boards.

Corporate Interrelationships

The three corporate boards do not overlap and they meet separately. This independence was created on advice of counsel to ensure separation and thereby protect the endowment assets. In addition, the foundation is to spend at least 10 percent of its endowment income on projects independent of the hospital. These funded proposals have included support for the regional volunteer ambulance corps, a retirement community, and an ambulatory care center at the periphery of the hospital's service area. Approximately 90 percent of the endowment income goes to the hospital for specific projects or to meet operating deficits.

Although the boards did not meet together, their minutes were shared and, as in any small town, members often knew each other and met outside the hospital.

For several years, this arrangement and corporate structure worked well, but with time the roles of the three boards became increasingly unclear:

Foundation Trustee: I see us as the corporate headquarters and the other organizations as subsidiaries.

Hospital Board Member: We run the hospital; we have a direct working knowledge of the hospital, while the foundation board does not. Their role is to manage the endowment assets and turn the interest over to us. That endowment was given to help the hospital.

For-Profit Board Member: At the moment we are a very small activity: we run a home health agency that breaks even. Our charter is to make money for the foundation and the hospital, but our home care agency provides a useful community service and should be continued, even if it does not make money. We also put on a statewide health conference, hoping to make a profit from it. However, we lost money and had to be reimbursed by the foundation, but that was before I was on this board.

Foundation Board Member: We see one of our roles as raising money for the hospital. However, no one knows our corporate name (The Regional Health Foundation) and they write checks to "Betterman Hospital" and the money goes to the hospital directly and is used for working capital. We also are empowered by the bylaws to do long-range planning. However, we have done little of that; we tend to respond to specific proposals for funds as they come to us.

New Problems

Last year the hospital board minutes reflected several important issues. A new contract with the physicians for emergency coverage, office space, and billing was being negotiated. A computer foul-up delayed billing for the hospital, creating a large bad debt. The hospital's cash position was supported by the sale of a gift to the hospital of a piece of property for $300,000, which was put into working capital. The national nursing shortage was felt locally, leading the hospital to approve a one-time large jump in nursing salaries and benefits. Although this would cause a deficit for the year after the outstanding bills were collected, the hospital board told the nurses that they would seek or get (the exact message remains unclear) money from the foundation to pay for this. The foundation trustees, after reading the hospital board minutes, came to the conclusion that the hospital was having serious problems, and they wanted an explanation.

First Foundation Trustee: The $300,000 should have come to the foundation and not stayed in the hospital. We would probably have added it to our endowment or loaned it to the hospital.

Second Foundation Trustee: We are responsible to the incorporators to be sure that our subsidiary corporations are being well managed.

Third Foundation Trustee: The hospital presented us with a demand for money to pay the nurses. They were making our decisions for us, when we are supposed to tell them what to do. We did not approve their request right away, but said we would think about it.

First Hospital Board Member: We explained in writing that the computer problem was temporary and being resolved. We think we are running the hospital responsibly. The foundation wants to meddle in hospital affairs about which they are not familiar.

Second Hospital Board Member: The foundation's problem is that they have nothing to do. Their endowment is managed by a Chicago bank. People originally gave that money to help the hospital. All the foundation should do is turn the interest over to the hospital. It's as simple as that.

Foundation Trustee: When we tabled the proposal for nurses' pay pending further discussion, the hospital board told the nurses that we refused their agreed-upon request for a pay raise. This makes us look like the bad guys and is irresponsible of the hospital board. They can promise anything, if someone else (that is us) pays for it.

The nurses invited the foundation trustee chairman to meet with them. He did so, explained the foundation's view, and obliquely implied that the hospital was being mismanaged. When the administrator and the hospital board chairman heard about this they were very upset. The hospital chairman wrote a letter to the foundation chairman saying that it was discourteous of him not to notify the hospital board about the meeting with the nurses and implying that it would be better if he stayed out of the hospital's affairs.

The Bylaws

The long-ignored bylaws of the three corporations—written in a rush in 1980—were brought out, dusted off, reproduced for the trustees and board members, and carefully read by all of them (mostly for the first time), only to show substantial ambiguity or complete silence on the several boards' responsibilities.

Two separate law firms were retained by the hospital and the foundation to interpret these bylaws. The foundation's lawyers said that the original distance between the corporations was no longer necessary. The hospital's lawyers urged that the distance be kept. The foundation chairman wrote to the hospital board chairman asking for a joint meeting of the two boards based on this advice. The hospital chairman refused to meet on the basis of their legal advice. A close reading of the several bylaws showed that any important interpretation or corporate change could be argued in court for a long (and expensive) time with the outcome unclear.

Except for the process of appointing trustees, the bylaws gave no advice about the relative roles of the corporations. Probably each corporation could change its own bylaws, but this was arguable.

Administrator: I would like this problem resolved, I sincerely would. It is taking up a lot of my time and staff time, which could be better spent elsewhere. The division of activity between the corporations could be made in a lot of different ways, and I could live with any one of them as long as there is agreement. I try and stay neutral and helpful, but it is difficult. Even so, depending on who wins this power struggle, my job is at risk. In a small town like this, these conflicts don't stay hidden long and become public knowledge, which would do us no good. I wish I knew how to resolve this.

Illustration 7.1 Betterman Memorial Hospital Corporate Structure Before and After 1980

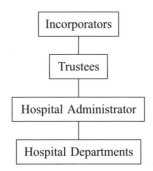

After 1980 and Corporate Reorganization

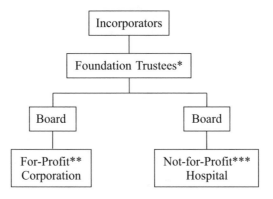

*The Regional Health Foundation, not-for-profit.
**The Regional Health Corporate Ventures, for-profit.
***Betterman Memorial Hospital, not-for-profit.

Changing Role of Stakeholders in the Delivery of Healthcare

Robert S. Curtis and Mary C. Morrison

Background

Northeastern Health Care System consists of a 450-bed acute care community hospital located in an urban area of the northeast. Included within the system is a 120-bed nursing home, a subacute service, home healthcare agency, hospice, various freestanding ancillary programs, physician practices, as well as an additional 120-bed long-term care facility under construction in an adjacent town.

The system is in an area where many hospitals are located offering similar and competing services. While it has a large, comprehensive medical staff, many of the doctors have privileges at other hospitals. Specialists dominate the medical staff in size and leadership.

Managed care companies were moving into the area and beginning to affect hospital and physician revenue as well as the delivery of healthcare. The system recognized that the healthcare industry was undergoing profound changes. What was once a cottage industry intent on meeting the everyday needs of its physicians and patients was being forced to resemble the for-profits and compete in a radically different environment.

As a result of market forces, the system could see a shift in emphasis from providing acute care to one that now focused on the continuum of healthcare. The same system that used to treat episodic illnesses of individuals was now expected to focus on the wellness of an entire defined population. The goal of filling beds was replaced by the objective to place the patient in a setting that would offer the appropriate level of care. What once was a medical center among many in the area was now one that needed to network with other providers to collaborate on common goals and objectives.

With such dynamic change taking place in an organization that in the past had functioned in a reasonably stable environment, the biggest challenge facing the system was anticipating and adapting to major shifts in the delivery of healthcare with substantially less in resources.

Situation

In response to these challenges, the medical center adopted a formal strategic planning process. A multidisciplinary committee was established that included board of trustees members, management, and physicians. The expectations of the committees were to:

- Reaffirm or modify the mission and philosophy statements;
- Identify strategic issues;
- Reach a consensus on long-term vision;
- Develop long-term goals in response to strategic issues;
- Establish key strategic objectives; and
- Provide a basis for management to develop key business strategies.

Two phases to this process were identified:

1. Develop a strategic direction/vision, and
2. Develop an action plan to achieve the strategic direction/vision.

Phase I consisted of answering two questions:

1. Where are we now? and
2. Where should we be going?

Phase II was intended to answer the question:

3. How are we going to get there?

Over the next several months the committee assessed the healthcare environment both regionally and nationally, and concluded that the traditional stand-alone acute care hospital was not going to be competitive in the future. They believed that the medical center needed to transform itself into a system that offered the community a continuum of healthcare services, ranging from primary to tertiary to post-hospital care.

To achieve this vision, the medical center recognized that it needed to develop approaches to address key strategic issues:

- Approach to the market
- Program/service initiatives
- Physician-hospital relations
- Service delivery accessibility
- Facility improvement
- Continuous quality improvement
- Community benefits.

Goals and objectives were established, followed by specific strategic actions required by management to accomplish the goals and objectives.

The board of trustees adopted the plan and charged management with its implementation. In addressing this charge management evaluated what it needed to do to carry out the objectives. A fundamental response was to redesign the organizational framework along the lines of the desired healthcare system components (i.e., managed care, integrated delivery systems, community services, etc.) (see Illustration 8.1, the organization chart).

As the plan unfolded, management pursued initiatives that included acquisition of physician practices, improved clinical and ancillary services, addition of outpatient services, and development of alternatives to acute care such as subacute and home health services. The result was the transformation of a hospital-centered organization into a sophisticated delivery system providing the community with a vertically integrated continuum of healthcare services.

The Medical Staff

The large medical staff (450) at Northeastern Health Care System, like those at similar institutions nationwide, were specialist-driven, in terms of both numbers and leadership. Hence, the increasing influence of managed care, characterized by declining physician income and restrictive practice, was a

Illustration 8.1 Redesigned Organization Structure Follows Strategy:

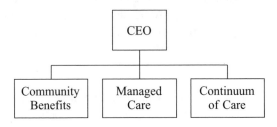

major assault on this group. As the economic and practice environment became more turbulent, the physicians became more anxious and sought to increase their influence within the health system as a means to control or, at best, minimize some of the impact of industry changes on them.

At Northeastern, physicians had for several years held more slots on the board of trustees than at any other area hospital. Furthermore, physicians were represented in every critical committee of the organization, chairing several. So it came as something of a surprise that as management pursued initiatives endorsed in the strategic plan, such as purchasing physician practices or developing specialty clinical services, the medical staff balked. The physicians viewed these and other activities as competition for them. During discussions with the medical staff leadership (all specialists), the physicians acknowledged participating in development of the strategic plan and recognized its long-term strategic importance to the system and its clinicians (although they believed it benefited primary care doctors over specialists). However, they would not embrace any ownership for the plan. They did not believe it adequately addressed individual physician needs and concerns relative to the assaults on their practices by the managed care environment.

As management sought to place the medical staff concerns in proper perspective, a single issue repeatedly came to the surface. Physicians clearly wanted a greater role in the decision-making process at all levels of the organization, from operations through governance, and they wanted that input at the level of issue identification.

The health system's operational CQI program had been functioning quite successfully with physicians participating on many committees and task forces. Management proposed that the physicians be given more opportunity for exposure to and influence in operations by integrating the medical staff and operating CQI programs. The proposal was adopted, the committee structures were integrated with physicians leading the new committees, and management and physicians agreed that this model was a meaningful collaborative activity.

The physicians, however, still sought more influence at the governing level and preferred to have that input outside of formal board meetings. In response, the board established ad hoc groups such as Building and Grounds committee and the Joint Conference committee composed of management, board, and physician leadership. As issues arose in these committees, additional ad hoc groups or information-gathering forums were introduced.

The Board

The board at Northeastern had reorganized several years ago with the health system parent board and the medical center board functioning as the primary governing bodies. Physicians, in addition to the medical staff officers, had been added representing both primary care and specialist backgrounds. Several new community members had replaced long-term retiring board members, and longstanding chairs have been replaced by younger board members.

The Northeastern board, like its neighboring counterparts, had traditionally been medical center–focused, assuring that the level of service provided in a traditional acute care facility met the needs of the community at high level. They grappled with the usual issues of financing, declining reimbursement, addition of new services and facilities, and filling empty beds.

The board spent considerable time educating themselves on the changing healthcare environment about managed care issues. They supported CQI as a core management strategy and had committed to the strategic plan as the foundation for ensuring organizational viability.

The board functioned through a committee structure that predated the strategic plan. The addition of several new ad hoc groups chartered to respond to physician views brought the number of board forums to 12 (see Illustration 8.1). On an ongoing basis the board oversaw the progress of the strategic plan through various committee reports. Information or issues discussed at the ad hoc group meetings were often referred to other ad hoc groups or board committees after management had prepared material relative to the subject matter.

The time commitments required by multiple meetings and the variety of issues the meetings raised, in addition to the amount of material presented, led several board members to feel overburdened. The traditional operating structure of the board caused it to be very issue-oriented, with a focus on singular internal items. This fostered an inward acute care medical center perspective and made it difficult for the board to operationalize its policy and planning role for an integrated health system.

Management

The executive management staff charged with implementing the strategic plan reorganized to focus on the core processes identified: Managed Care, Integrated Delivery Systems, and Community Services. Reporting relationships and responsibilities drastically changed as each of these core process groups sought to create the infrastructure necessary to realize its particular goals. In addition to managed care contracting, the Managed Care division sought to build a primary care network. A primary care network was a key strategy for bringing to the system large numbers of covered lives, and was to be accomplished through the acquisition of new practices or practice acquisition from retiring physicians. Other practice arrangements would also be pursued.

Given the financial challenges posed by severely discounted managed care contracts, the Integrated Delivery System division sought to move the patient seamlessly across the continuum. This necessitated new and different operating systems, revised systemwide job descriptions, salary structures, and so on, and a focus beyond hospital-based acute care to other modes of patient care delivery. Acute care services needed to focus on the primary clinical strengths of the organization. While many of the requirements of an integrated delivery system would be addressed through functional and operational changes, the transition in organizational thinking and perspective presented the most significant challenge.

Community Services sought first to identify the community's health status and its real and desired health needs and then to design and implement community-based programming to improve healthcare outcomes. Much of the community healthcare up until this time had been delivered from the fee-for-service episodic illness perspective in a solo practice physician's office.

Each of these core integrated system processes required significantly different activities than it had ever before embraced. These activities, carried out in an environment where physicians were economically threatened, led to almost consistent physician challenge of every system initiative.

Primary care development required the system's acquisition and operation of physician practices in areas where it was believed market share could be gained. Physicians viewed these capital-intensive initiatives as competition to them and as diversion of scarce financial resources from the acute care medical center.

Moving patients across the integrated continuum depended on intensive care management. While many physicians believed case management was supportive to their practice, the stringent application of utilization guidelines and the intervention of multiple professionals was often seen as an intrusion on the doctor-patient relationship and as a restriction of practice autonomy.

Community Health initiatives were also seen by the physician as competition, since many of the community-based solo practitioners believed that they already adequately met the community's healthcare needs.

As management sought to move ahead with the strategic agenda, physician leadership sought increased input and involvement in the belief that initiatives could be pursued in a manner or a modified form that did not displease any member of the medical staff. In some cases, they sought to halt the initiatives altogether. The board, sympathetic to physicians' concerns, formed ad hoc forums to investigate or pursue alternative or modified options.

Management staffed these ad hoc forums and did most of the work associated with achieving the agenda. Management also continued to involve physicians in multiple planning and meetings in attempts to modify strategic initiatives from a consensus-building framework. The result, from management's perspective, was that the strategic plan was not moving forward with the clarity and intensity required to be successful.

As it sought to respond to physician concerns, management was receiving mixed messages from the board as the management team was directed to revisit and reassess previous commitments to strategic initiatives. The additional work associated with staffing multiple board forums, coupled with the ad hoc specific-issue orientation of the board, resulted in a frustrated operational gridlock for management. It also resulted in confusion by the stakeholders regarding who was providing the organization with direction from a systemwide community perspective.

The CEO

The CEO had guided the organization's growth successfully for the past 15 years. He was fully committed to following the strategic plan as the road map to the organization's future viability. By organizing a management team with the necessary skills and experience, he was able to move the organization along the strategic path adopted by the board. As a result he had earned and enjoyed an excellent working relationship with the board and had been able to work successfully with the medical staff. Over the course of several years, the CEO had increased the interaction between executive management and the board members to the point that the board felt quite secure in the capabilities of the management team.

As the strategic plan implementation strategies unfolded in a highly competitive environment, the CEO found that more of his time was devoted to listening and responding to physician concerns, interpreting individual physician issues to board members, and attempting to place these issues within a system context. He spent considerable time, too, working with the management staff to develop or modify initiatives in response to board ad hoc committee recommendations.

With little time to position the organization in a managed care environment, the CEO and the management staff were increasingly frustrated by bottlenecks that resulted from restudying and revisiting issues and objectives. In addition, both board members and medical staff leaders began to express similar frustrations, voicing concern that the organization no longer had a clear vision for the future. The CEO recognized that while significant activity was going on (see Illustration 8.2), the organization was not moving forward to position itself for managed care. An analysis of the organization's leadership roles was rapidly becoming essential as the organization drifted in conflicting directions.

Illustration 8.2   Current Restructured Board Committees

CURRENT BOARD COMMITTEES

Executive/Finance
Strategic Planning
Quality Improvement
Joint Conference
Board Development
Facilities
Risk
Bioethics
Long-Term Care
Community Benefits

SUBCOMMITTEES

Retirement
Pastoral Care

RESTRUCTURED COMMITTEES

Board	Management
Executive/Finance	Long-Term Care
Strategic Planning	Risk Management
Quality Improvement	Facilities Development
Board Development	Bioethics
Joint Conference	Pastoral Care

Part **IV**

Professional Integration

Introduction

The power of physicians and nurses has changed over the decades of this century, and not in unison. Before the Flexner reforms, starting in 1910, a few months of education would qualify one to become a physician and there were lots of hungry physicians. In 1910, it was possible for a nurse or physician to say as a joke, "I had a good practice, but my patient died." A wealthy patient could and did pay for a full-time physician or private duty nurse. As medical schools were closed following the Flexner reforms, there was a long delay in reducing the number of practitioners. Many physicians struggled during the depression, while hospital administrators took big pay cuts to hold their jobs. The growth of health insurance after World War II led to a golden era of medicine. Nursing education largely moved out of the hospital and into the college and university. Cost-based reimbursement of Medicare and Blue Cross could support the growth of hospitals and their staff.

In this postwar era, the power of physicians was great. The most likely reason a hospital administrator would lose his job was because the medical staff wanted to get rid of him. Physicians, not pleased with the hospital, could often easily shift their admissions to another nearby hospital. The hospital would add new equipment and services to attract specialists. One reaction to the rising costs that resulted has been prospective payment (DRGs), capitation (HMOs, PPOs), and price competition between managed care plans. The HMOs have discovered how to provide care with fewer hospitals, fewer hospital beds, smaller staff, and fewer doctors and nurses. Downsizing in hospitals in the late 1990s has become routine, leading to an abundance of nurses compared to the positions available. The effects of competitive managed care on the need for doctors is beginning to be felt, particularly for specialists. What will be the steady state for physician supply and demand? A diversion into labor economics is needed to predict this future. Physicians and nurses will not earn the incomes of some professional athletes whose presence at a game can sell more tickets, popcorn, and souvenirs. The pay of stars can be linked to their drawing power. The other extreme is the fast food restaurant, like McDonalds, which provides the same hamburger in 80 or more countries largely using minimum wage part-time labor. McDonalds management has done this by designing a working environment that makes it nearly impossible to make a bad batch of french fries.

Nursing and medicine will fall within these extremes of income and power. A good physician, nurse, and primary care practice can draw patients like a magnet. If this group can attract 3,000 new subscribers to an HMO at $120 per member per month, that creates a gross income for their HMO of ($3,000 x 120 x 12) or $4,320,000. Care teams that patients brag about are economically valuable to the HMO. Conversely, specialists may only cost money rather than attract new enrollees. The result is a shift in the balance of power between primary and specialty care. The successful managed care plan wants to attract these "platinum" primary care provider groups. It wants to educate them to improve their practice and it wants to retain them.

This is played out in the two cases in this section. The "Electronic Physician Practice" case shows the process of improving practice organization driven by an internal manager. The "Primary Care Instrumental Panel" case shows the process from the perspective of the managed care plan.

Excellence in primary care means not only finding good practitioners, but also surrounding them in a practice setting that works flawlessly to delight patients and meet their care needs appropriately. Organizing this practice environment is a vital role for the health manager.

The medical profession retains its basic and legally enforced monopoly over the key functions of healthcare, as physicians are the sole authority in diagnosing and carrying out the treatment of health problems. The basis of their decision making has been experience and clinical judgment. Increasingly, this informal, unchallengeable mode of decision making is being replaced by "evidence-based medicine," based on good evidence of effectiveness, population-based reasoning, clinical decision analysis, cost-effectiveness analysis, utilization review, clinical paths, guidelines or algorithms, process improvement thinking, outcomes, health status and quality of life measurements and comparative cost analysis.

In dealing with physicians, the manager must remember that physicians vary in their dependence on the organization for income, tenure, power, and status. Increasingly, physicians are members of hospital boards or employed by hospitals in administrative positions.

Physicians can rely on numerous sources of power in dealing with managers, including the protection afforded them by organizations and medical staff bylaws or through negotiated contracts. Physicians may use the authority based on their knowledge of medicine to demand resources from the manager such as additional staff, space, and equipment. Physicians are often respected by nurses and other employees. They may have access to board members and community leaders who are their patients. Their power may stem from the ability to enlist the support of other physicians as a group or from their lack of dependence on a specific institution for referral of patients.

Physicians expect recognition, acceptance, and trust from the manager, and they expect that their livelihoods will not be threatened by managerial initiative. Physicians are concerned about their status and power compared to other occupational groups—other physicians within the organization, and physicians practicing at competing institutions. They want to determine their own working conditions and to be provided with support services adequate to house, feed, and care for their patients. Physicians do not like to waste time in endless or frequent meetings, and they expect to be consulted if organizational policy changes will affect them.

Many of these seem reasonable expectations. Why, then, does the physician feel that expectations are not met by the organization and the manager? Other physicians may be competing for limited resources of funds, space, and staff; demand may change for one specialty compared to others. The manager may have a different concept of time wasting. Completing records represents time unreimbursed to the physician, but a necessary cash flow to the hospital. Sometimes events move too quickly for adequate consultation or there is a lack of communication between medical officials and staff physicians.

For instance, a manager may ask the chief of staff, a department head, or the medical board for approval of implementation of a risk management program, provision of financial guarantees to recruit general practitioners, or appointment of a new chief of emergency medicine. Medical officials may give informal approval and wish to get back to physicians in each department for further discussion and recommendations for action. In the interim, however, time, money, and skilled personnel may disappear. Even after policies exist, the manager often finds that physicians have misinterpreted medical officials at staff meetings, or have misread the committee minutes. Following implementation of new policies, physicians may personally object and subsequently practice a poor quality of medicine. Yet they fail to understand why their peers do not always honor their legitimate requests. Further, a physician's interests may conflict with organizational goals.

Similarly, the manager expects recognition, acceptance, and trust from physicians. She expects physicians to be concerned about organizational goals such as cost containment and quality improvement. The manager expects the physician to fulfill specific organizational commitments agreed to in advance, such as punctual attendance at committee meetings of the medical board the physician chairs. The manager does not expect to be attacked personally when she and a physician disagree about an issue. She expects respect for management's organizational role, that is, the coordination of activities within the organization and adaptation of the organization to environmental pressures. The manager expects the physician not to waste the manager's time but, for example, to try to solve a problem first with a department head whose lack of a timely response to the physician's request may be reasonable. The manager expects to be consulted if an action by a medical official or attending physician will affect the organization's goal attainment or system maintenance.

Many of these seem reasonable expectations. Why then don't physicians meet them? Physicians may not view the manager as she views herself. Physicians may view the manager as a supporter of clinical services rather than as a coordinator or integrator. They may see the manager as working *for* them rather than *with* them to attain organizational goals. Many physicians may fear the manager because of increasing dependence on the organization for their livelihood. Managers, through their influence on budget determination and their control of information, may affect the physician's access to scarce resources.

In the cases in this section, if physicians can discredit the manager, the manager will have less power over them. Physicians are accustomed to giving orders, not taking them. If the manager is actively attempting to increase revenues and decrease expenses, physicians can surely find fault. (The manager did not consult sufficiently with them, she did not consult sufficiently in advance, or she has favored certain departments in budget and staff.) Further, physicians might object to the manager's tone, style, travel schedule, number of assistants hired, size of office, or amount of salary.

Physicians will often disagree with the manager over policy. For example, physicians at one hospital may decide that expensive equipment will help in their daily practice, and surgeons at a neighboring hospital are getting more sophisticated equipment. The former hospital's policy of providing services to the chronically ill will therefore not help surgeons stay competitive or increase their incomes. Or physicians may have a conflict of interest with the hospital; given a certain amount of radiology revenues, for instance, more money for the radiologist may mean less for the hospital, and vice versa.

There is no effective organizational responsibility system for most physician behavior. Physicians can take "cheap shots" at the manager if they are not effectively accountable to anyone in the organizational structure for incurring costs or ensuring quality and access. Non-paid physician department chiefs and committee chairs are usually more interested in maintaining their physician networks of patient referral than in attaining organizational goals. Physicians work long hours and they consider the competing and conflicting demands on their time more important than certain organizational obligations, even those to which they have agreed in advance.

Finally, physicians may distrust the manager, find the manager incompetent, or dislike the manager personally. This may be because of the manager's actions or inactions, ranging from gaining board approval for a CT scanner to responding appropriately to low nursing morale.

Given the inherent difficulties, what opportunities do managers have to perform effectively and yet maintain decent working relationships with physicians? Is this even possible? Managers can exchange scarce resources of money, staff, and space with physicians in return for assistance in goal attainment. Managers can order physicians to implement decisions, calculating that physicians lack the power to resist effectively. Managers can persuade physicians to act in the long-term interest of the organization, the patient, and the consumer. The manager has a limited amount of political "chips" to spend, just as she has a limited amount of money available. The manager can invest in political power by building good informal relationships with key physicians, or she can spend power in making decisions opposed by key physicians or groups. Timing, tone, body language, and judgment are all important for the manager whose tenure may well vary conversely with activism.

The manager has resources available that the physician lacks. She may have influence with the governing board regarding long-range planning decisions; influence on appointment of physicians to paid and unpaid positions; access to grants and gifts; and influence on physician reimbursement. The manager is in a position to advise physicians on business and personal problems and to do personal favors for them. The manager has information concerning workable implementation of her ideas at other hospitals and health centers.

Even as the physician has medical authority for patient care decisions, the manager has authority based on expertise in marketing and government regulation. Often competitive and regulatory requirements can be interpreted by managers to rationalize decisions that will benefit patients and consumers at the expense or inconvenience of physicians. The manager may also accrue a certain authority by virtue of long tenure in the position, having gained the trust of physicians with similar tenure. When a manager has gained such trust, others will back critical decisions or disagree in private or in advance, without personally attacking.

The manager can persuade physicians of the justice or advantage of policy or administrative decisions. Of course, some physicians will not wish to be persuaded. It is not difficult to wake up someone who is sleeping, but it's very hard to awaken someone who is pretending to be asleep.

The manager can help physicians obtain the resources they need, which may be in the organization's interest as well. The manager may avoid what physicians oppose until a more favorable future time, if ever. Above all, the manager must know what she is doing, be sure of her facts, and be conservative in her forecasts. As in other fields, nothing succeeds like success or fails like failure, and often the failing manager will not be given a second chance.

The two cases, "The 'Electronic' Physician Practice" and the "Primary Care Instrument Panel," approach the same problem from different directions. The problem is to move toward the use of computers to generate practice information on costs, types, and volume of services and outcomes. In the first case, the desire for change is being given from within the group practice by a manager. In the second case, the effort is coming from the corporate headquarters of the managed care plan. Both cases are concerned with bringing along the physicians. In the long run these changes will occur. The problem is how to get from here to there, sooner than later.

Case Questions

The "Electronic" Physician Practice

- What should Joan recommend that the board do, given the present situation?
- What constraints and opportunities does the board face in attempting to implement Joan's recommendations?
- What should Joan do if the board is not willing to accept her main recommendations in the areas of information technology, finance, personnel, and marketing?
- What kind of progress can Joan reasonably expect from the board over the next year?

The Primary Care Instrument Panel

- Design the physician "instrument panel."
- What should be in it?
- Justify why you would include these components. Think about how costly it would be to obtain this information.
- What is needed to get your goal of an appropriate instrument panel? (Just defining the ideal does not get you there.)
- Design a "just-in-time" education program to respond to requests from physician groups.
- What topics should be covered? List these topics.
- For a high priority topic, outline the content of the educational module.

Selected Bibliography

Accreditation Manual for Hospitals, 1996 Edition. Chicago: Joint Commission on Accreditation of Healthcare Organizations, 1995.

Altman, Stuart, and Uwe E. Reinhardt (eds.). *Strategic Choices for a Changing Health Care System*. Chicago: Health Administration Press, 1996.

Davidson, Stephen M., et al. *The Physician Manager Alliance: Building the Health Care Organization*. San Francisco: Jossey-Bass, 1996.

Delbecq, Andre, and Sandra L. Gill. "Justice as a Prelude to Teamwork in Medical Centers." *Health Care Management Review* 10 no. 1 (winter 1985): 45–51.

Edwards, Janine C., and Robert M. Donati. *Medical Practice in the Current Health Care Environment: A Handbook for Residents and Medical Students*. Baltimore, MD: Johns Hopkins University Press, 1995.

Freidson, Eliot. *Medical Work in America*. New Haven, CT: Yale University Press, 1989.

———. *Professionalism Reborn*. Chicago: University of Chicago Press, 1984.

Mechanic, David. *Inescapable Decisions: The Imperatives of Health Reform*. New Brunswick, NJ: Transaction Publishers, 1994.

Shortell, Stephen, et al. *Remaking Health Care in America: Building Organized Delivery Systems*. San Francisco: Jossey-Bass, 1996.

Wirth, Todd S., and Seth Allcorn. *Creating New Hospital-Physician Collaboration*. Chicago: Health Administration Press, 1993.

Wolf, Stewart. *Educating Doctors: Crisis in Medical Education, Research and Practice*. New Brunswick, NJ: Transaction Press, 1997.

Case **9**

The "Electronic" Physician Practice from Fee-for-Service to Managed Care

Joan Kiel

Between 1984 and 1994, inpatient admissions decreased 12.6 percent. During that same ten-year period, outpatient visits increased 80.7 percent.[1] With this influx of patients in outpatient settings, today's physician office is very different from that of the past—even of the recent past, one or two years ago. Because of this, both physicians and their staffs must implement changes.

In the past, the physician was accustomed to autonomy, entrepreneurship, and the rewards that accompanied hard work. The more time one put in, the more patients one saw, the more income one could expect. Physicians formed collegial networks, which made referrals seem like a social call to a buddy. Patients' demands were met as the physicians and their staff made every attempt to appease and retain their clientele. Pleasing service and satisfied patients meant more referrals, more visits, higher volumes of service, and thus greater income. The incentives were based on a volume-income relationship. Few problems emerged, but perhaps all good things must come to an end.

Enter the mid-1990s, the era of managed care: the autonomy has eroded, the entrepreneurship rationale is questioned, and the rewards are measured differently. No longer do physicians have control of their income without first validating procedures and visits with a utilization review manager or against a clinical pathway. Referrals are now made within a structured managed care organization network, and scrutinized for their utility. Quality assurance audits ensure that appropriate care is given, but capitation fees also ensure that costs remain in control. Physicians must balance the number of patients with what diagnoses to treat. No longer is the volume-income relationship true.

Patients need to change behaviors and enhance compliance for healthier lifestyles. Doctors and their staff are working to monitor appropriate office utilization while simultaneously providing customer service. Offices are also asked by managed care organizations for financial and clinical data that are time-consuming to gather and questioned regarding their purpose. The physician-patient relationship and medical privacy have been overshadowed by the managed care network. The result of this has been decreased physician salaries and increases in mergers and physician buyouts by insurance companies and hospitals—and an office staff deluged with more work. The worst is that the change is in its infancy. Outpatient visits will continue to surpass inpatient admissions; managed care organizations will continue to demand information. What does this mean for physician practice in terms of implementing change to meet the demands of managed care?

A Practice in Transition

Joan Marone is the office manager of a four-physician, 27,000 patient practice located 12 miles from Pittsburgh. She manages one family practice office with a staff of 22 (two full-time registered nurses, one part-time licensed practical nurse, four full-time medical assistants, six part-time medical assistants, two full-time front desk personnel, three full-time telephone personnel, one full-time records manager, and three full-time billers and coders). (See Illustration 9.1: Organization Chart). The office is open six days a week, including four evenings until 9:00 p.m. The patients range from infants to elderly persons with a total population of 24,000. Ninety percent come from within a ten-mile radius with the remaining 10 percent coming from up to 22 miles. Within a 20-mile radius are 14 hospitals, 190 family practice and internal medicine physicians, and three major managed care organizations.

The office has been open for 17 years. It started with one physician and three years later added a second; five years ago a third was added, and three months ago the fourth was added; all are males. The three oldest are board-certified in family practice and the fourth is board-eligible. All of the physicians work 4.5 days per week.

Joan Marone is preparing for the annual board meeting of the practice. Her biggest concern is the onslaught of managed care in the area. She once thought that it was "something that only happened in California," but now she sees increasingly more mergers, physician practice buyouts, and insurance plans. Joan and the physicians have rarely worried until now about managed care. Patients keep coming in, bills are being paid, and the staff is content. But

Illustration 9.1   Group Practice Organization Chart

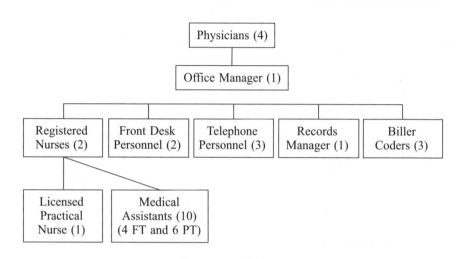

now they realize that in the future one cannot just exist, one must capitalize on opportunity. The practice must behave strategically in order to remain competitive.[2]

The Influx of Managed Care

A two-to-three–page document has changed the healthcare industry—the managed care contract. Joan Marone has found that this document has major implications for physician practices in management information systems, finance, personnel, and marketing. She hears from her colleagues that managed care, with its call for a coordinated continuum of care, will increase demands for business principles, financial acumen, and information technology. She also believes, though, that the result will be increased efficiency and effectiveness and a competitive edge for the practice. She knows that there will be many changes. She wonders about her own job security, the onslaught of managed care organizations, and the reaction of the physicians. With all of these issues, what will take precedent? Not wanting to wait to find out, she sets out to prepare and plan for the board meeting.

Management Information Systems (MIS)

When one walks into Marone's physician practice, one sees everything from a manual check-in system to an array of computer terminals (Illustration 9.2).

Even with a plethora of terminals, one cannot assume that this is positively correlated with a sophisticated, efficient system. Further examination of the computer arrangement reveals that one is for scheduling appointments, another for managed care referrals, a third for word processing, and two for coding and billing. There exists no practice management information systems (PMIS)— the integration of the terminals. Mrs. Marone wonders about this since she has seen advertisements for a PMIS that can track patients across the continuum of care—from the home where the person may utilize home care and pharmacy services, to the physician practice, to the hospital where the person may undergo routine tests, procedures, and consults. She has heard that information tracked and monitored across the continuum will help to achieve the goal of managed care: providing quality, cost-effective care. Another advantage of a PMIS is that it can communicate with a data repository.

She sets out to analyze and to reach conclusions about her needs. A major concern is cash collections as the office's 90-plus day balance is above average. The physicians have instituted a policy that they will not see patients who have an outstanding balance greater than 90 days. Implementing this policy has been difficult to do because, when scheduling, the telephone personnel do not have access to the accounts payable records. They simply rely on the patient's word. Last month 113 patients were treated who had balances greater than 90 days, amounting to $7,910. The office's collection procedures are fruitless if people know that they can continue to schedule despite having a balance. Joan needs an information system that can track these balances and be readily available to the schedulers.

Joan Marone has requested to meet with a PMIS representative to discuss how the various office functions can be electronically integrated. She has heard about Windows-based systems that can simultaneously display scheduling and

Illustration 9.2 Office Layout

			Entrance (Check-In)			
Office Manager	Scheduling	Checkout	Exam 1 Room	Exam 2 Room	Exam 3 Room	Exam 4 Room
Files	Supplies					
Break Room	Billers and Coders	Medication Room	Exam 5 Room	Exam 6 Room	Exam 7 Room	Exam 8 Room

billing functions. This would allow those with greater than a 90-day balance to be blocked from scheduling. Joan is also interested in a patient database that will track a variety of demographic and socioeconomic factors. The physicians have been asking her about Internet access, which would allow them to do on-line research and to communicate with colleagues and perhaps even patients. She is also open to other suggestions that the representative will have. With the onslaught of managed care, information systems become all the more critical.

Cost Analysis and Managed Care Contracts

Joan Marone is well aware that financial implications are paramount with managed care. She has continually heard from the physicians that to make more money, not only must one work more but one must also carefully assess the plethora of managed care contracts. All too often contracts are "signed and filed" without the realization that the managed care organization will determine the practice's compensation via capitation. Thus, the amount of money spent to produce an outcome should be known exactly—what did the physical examination cost to produce? What are the inputs and costs for each procedure? Here the manager must track the cost of the procedure and compare it to the capitation rate of *each* managed care contract. Mrs. Marone knows that doing this for every office procedure for every managed care contract will be cumbersome, but what is she to do to appease the physicians and stabilize the practice? In the future, she would like to have a PMIS perform the cost analyses.

Joan instructs her staff that she will be conducting cost analyses and thus will be requesting data. She begins by identifying the ten most frequent procedures and diagnoses handled by the office:

1. Physical examination (Male 16–19)
2. Pap smear
3. Physical examination (Male 55–60)
4. Gastritis
5. Common cold
6. Electrocardiogram (Male 45–49)
7. Low back pain
8. Childhood immunizations
9. Influenza
10. Headache

Now she will need to calculate how much it has been costing to provide each service or treat each of the above diagnoses. A good electronic system can calculate a fee analysis for each diagnosis and correlate it with age, gender, zip code, physician, and various other factors. After completing the fee analysis, it can be downloaded to produce updated reports, whether every day, every week, or every month.[3] Having a PMIS would electronically keep the information current as fees fluctuate. Also the PMIS would calculate the variance from the capitation rates to assess the efficiency of the office's performance. But without the PMIS, Joan manually tallies personal wages, supplies, overhead, and equipment depreciation for each of the ten diagnoses. As she does this, her other work is piling up.

Managed care also demands that the practice manager know what types of patients use what procedures and then to determine the profit margin for each, for as harsh as it sounds, offices need to "balance" the types of patients seen with the procedures completed to maintain profits. Joan is gathering data to compile this information, but again she is doing it manually. She realizes that a PMIS can determine benchmarks for the adequate number of patients and procedures needed to maintain profits. On the other hand, she wonders if the PMIS will complicate office life.

The physicians are inquiring if Mrs. Marone is monitoring for "contract skimming"? This occurs when the monthly capitation checks are progressively slightly less that the negotiated rates. If a contract if signed and filed in a drawer, or if the office uses a manual system, the paper can be overwhelming and the manager never notices a difference in payment. Joan has started to assess this, but on a manual basis it has become difficult. She realizes that with a PMIS, the cost of services rendered for each managed care contract can be calculated and then compared with the negotiated fees. Also, claims denied by an insurer can be assessed. Denial rates become more critical at contract renewal time, but it is useful to track them throughout the life of the contract. Maintaining this information in a database is the most logical and effective method, given the multiple managed care contracts that physicians sign. All contracts must be assessed in terms of their profitability. At the month's end, offices will soon be printing out the "Wall Street Journal of data." The physicians are getting impatient for reports. Joan feels that the data needs are becoming a burden.

The physicians also inform Joan that she needs to collect data that track utilization of services by patient mix, managed care payor, and physician. Data need to be collected on hospital length of stay and clinical occurrences (including illnesses, medications used, and procedures completed) by demographics. This allows the physicians to follow what types of patients are spending how much money on what services. It also allows the physicians to benchmark against each other.

An information system is also needed to generate a list of limited services (i.e., a dental visit every six months), thus preventing a patient from scheduling sooner and being billed. Verification from managed care companies for providing services can occur electronically, thus allowing physicians faster turnaround times. Managed care organizations that are computerized can communicate with "electronic" offices to track referrals, procedures, and costs. Joan knows that her office will look and operate very differently in the future. Managed care will dictate this and it is her responsibility to implement the best office protocols.

Personnel

Although Joan is aware of the operational changes that need to occur with managed care, she is additionally hesitant now because the practice has been involved in merger discussions. She knows that this will present both opportunities and problems. Physicians may be granted more favorable managed care rates, but Joan is most worried about merging positions and personalities, and the possibility of downsizing, including herself, due to duplication of roles. On the other hand, personnel functions will multiply to include related fields such as employee development and organizational change, for which Joan must be trained. As the practices integrate, cultures, missions, and goals will also need to merge. Practices that fail to see the importance of this early on will face tremendous growing pains.

Also on the personnel side, Joan Marone is well aware that the information explosion has made great demands for data from managed care organizations and for cost controls from doctors. Additional skills in information technology and finance will need to be learned. Positions such as data collectors, data entry specialists, system designers, programmers, and costs specialists will be needed. In the past Marone has considered outsourcing the work because many times it is less expensive than adding multiple people with exact skills. She will need to undergo that personal debate again.

If Joan chooses not to outsource, formal education and on-the-job training will be needed for herself and her staff. With so much information, it must be somebody's responsibility within the practice to organize the necessary data. She cannot assume this to be a small task, for it is hardly that. While in small offices, data organization is often just one of the many roles that a person is responsible for, in larger, merged practices, a full-time person is needed.

Human resources, along with Joan, will also be involved in retraining or hiring for the other new duties related to managed care. This becomes even more crucial if her office becomes involved in a merger, because information will have to flow between physically disparate office sites. She is also well aware that information technology means that functions such as scheduling, billing, and coding can be done electronically—which would reduce her staff in these areas.

Marketing

Another impact that Mrs. Marone faces is the marketing of the practice. She has heard that no longer will marketing be dependent on "glossy brochures," but rather on data-laden information that depicts proper utilization, patient satisfaction, and lowered costs. This is what managed care organizations are most interested in, not pictures of fancy waiting rooms or larger suites. Here Joan Marone must change her marketing mindset. The audience now becomes not only the patient/consumer, but also the managed care company. Because of this, she knows her practice must change the way it records, analyzes, and presents data. It now becomes everyone's responsibility. All of the data that she has been previously collecting manually can be used for marketing purposes. She also knows that with a PMIS, the data can be formatted into a brochure. She begins to realize that the "electronic" office may be a lifesaver in this era of the information explosion and managed care.

Joan must begin now to prepare for the annual board meeting. She knows that this year's agenda will be very different from that of last year. Physicians are questioning their salaries, the new buzzwords, and the onslaught of office changes brought about by managed care. Joan and her staff must be able to provide the information being demanded by managed care organizations. She knows that she must implement change as other offices have, but the hectic office pace leaves little time to plan. People tell her that with a committed staff, modern information technology, and education in managed care, the office will prosper. Joan is skeptical; there is just so much to do. She now seeks out her staff for help in preparing for the annual meeting.

The physicians have informed her that they wish to discuss the following questions:

- What should Joan Marone recommend that the board do, given the present situation?
- What constraints and opportunities does the board face in attempting to implement Joan's recommendations?
- What should Joan do if the board is not willing to accept her main recommendations in the areas of information technology, finance, personnel, and marketing?
- What kind of progress can Joan reasonably expect from the board over the next year?

Notes

1. *American Hospital Association Statistics and Trends, 1995.* xxvii. (Chicago: American Hospital Association, 1996).
2. Douglas A. Bender, and Carla J. Krasnick, *Medical Practice Management* (Sept/Oct 1995): 54.
3. Dennis Murray, "Keep Your Eyes from Being Squeezed." *Medical Economics* (12 June 1995): 47.

The Primary Care Instrument Panel at Central Community Health Plan

Duncan Neuhauser

Two student teams are doing a field elective project under the supervision of Peter Alexander, M.D., who is chief medical officer and chief operating officer of Central Community Health Plan (CCHP). Central Community is a managed care plan with 500,000 enrollees in an area with a population of 2.5 million people, and is by far the largest health plan in the area.

The teams each include a medical student, nursing student, and health management student, all of whom are enrolled in an interdisciplinary course on continuous quality improvement (CQI) in healthcare. The teams are expected to work on a problem assigned to them: to understand the process and causes of variation, and to plan an improvement to this process.

Dr. Alexander finished his residency in general internal medicine the week before he started this job at Central Community Health Plan (CCHP), turning down several similar positions to choose this one. Before starting his residency, he worked for the Hospital Corporation of America. He did his residency on a half-time basis. While doing so, he developed a successful consulting company advising physician groups about managed care.

Peter: CCHP now contracts with 3,000 independent providers who are mostly physicians in our service area. We have contracts with 22 hospitals in the area, which account for about a third of the total in the area. These contracted hospitals agree to provide care at low prices, agree to participate in utilization review, and have reputations for good care. The physicians also have contracts defining the prices they charge for services and agreeing to utilization review. CCHP has revenue and expenses of about $2 billion a year.

Student: All over town, hospitals and physician groups are being purchased and being grouped together as systems of care competing with each other. Do you plan to do this?

Peter: We have three choices. First, we could buy hospitals, group practices, nursing homes, pharmacies, home care organizations, and such. A lot of capital would be tied up in this approach, but we would have more direct control.

Our second choice is to buy nothing, but contract with independent physicians, hospitals, and other providers. In this case, our organization will be small in staff. I envision a corporate headquarters of about 50 people for this $2–3 billion corporation. Our corporate staff will consist of physicians, practice management consultants, management information system managers, quality improvement coaches, and people who write contracts with providers and employer groups. The value added, based on the relatively small capital invested (compared to owning hospitals), would be great.

The third choice would be a mix of one and two. If the opportunity or need arose to own a provider corporation, we could buy it. We would take a mixed approach, depending on the circumstances. Of these three, we are taking the second approach for now.

Student: Is this wise? Why wouldn't the providers create their own managed care plan and go directly to the payers, thereby passing CCHP entirely? In a sense, HMOs like Kaiser Permanente do this.

Peter: HMOs like Kaiser Permanente have a different set of strengths and weaknesses and a role to play. We think there is a larger role for a plan like CCHP.

We are planning to select about 800 primary care providers out of our 3,000 providers and to work with them closely. We call this core group our "platinum providers." The 800 physicians are members of 90 group practices. They will have an opportunity to own part of CCHP. We will provide them with expert advice on improving their practice. We will provide an information system in support of their practice. This will have several components. It will eliminate their back office paperwork related to billing. The patient's Master or VISA card or CCHP member card "swiped" by a machine reader will bring up the patient's record, record the care provider, and make billing from plan to provider automatic. The patient's self-pay component will be coped with before the patient leaves the office.

We plan to have a council of expert medical advisers to bring the latest knowledge to our partnership. Our staff is prepared to assess the group's readiness for managed care and to give advice on improving market share, improving office practice, analyzing competitors, and planning. We plan to be able to provide these groups with accounting support, information systems, and group purchasing with the goal of reducing the percentage of the group's income that goes to office expense from the current 55 percent to 35 percent. We plan to have the capacity to develop "clinical profiling" for individual physicians and groups and for all our plan members. These include:

1. Pathophysiological outcomes (for example, average blood sugar level for your diabetics);
2. Patient satisfaction;
3. Functional health status (for example, sickness days);
4. Future patient health risk (for example, percent of appropriate patients who have had mammography); and
5. Cost to payer of plan—both direct and indirect (for the XYZ corporation, the costs per employee and family member, both medical care costs and other company costs such as sickleave days).

These measures will be the basis for data displayed on our physician instrument panel.

Student: What is an instrument panel?

Peter: It's like flying an airplane. What "real time" information should a primary care provider have to be able to manage his or her practice superbly? Our goal is to have ready access to the information needed to measure costs, quality, and satisfaction for the physician's panel of providers at CCHP. Here is an outline of one (see Illustration 10.1).

Student: Will you pay the doctors more if they have better satisfaction scores than others? Will you punish those with worse scores? I know of a managed care plan where doctors get $10,000 end-of-year bonuses for very satisfied patients and lose $10,000 if their patients are dissatisfied.

Peter: What would be Dr. Edwards Deming's answer to that question? Our whole idea is to be partners with physicians, not to punish them and not to own them. They have suffered too much from unthinking, venal managed care plans. We want to be different.

When we meet next week, I want one student team to present me with the information that should be in our primary care instrument panel. Here are some ideas. Illustration 10.2 shows some information that will help us track our comparative costs.

You might also think about the HEDIS measures. As you know, these are the performance measures that employer-payers judge us on. They expect us to have this information. The HEDIS data are changing but will continue to include such measures as (1) the percentage of the elderly who've had influenza immunizations; (2) the percentage of women of the appropriate age ranges who have had a pap smear and mammography; (3) the percentage of

Illustration 10.1   Template for an Instrument Panel Displaying Inputs
(Patient Case-Mix Variables), Clinical Process Vari-
ables, and Outputs (Clinical Outcomes, Functional
Outcomes, Patient Satisfaction, and Cost and
Utilization).

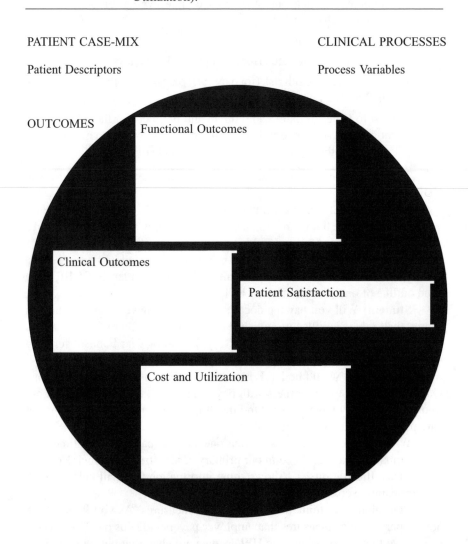

PATIENT CASE-MIX   CLINICAL PROCESSES

Patient Descriptors   Process Variables

OUTCOMES

Functional Outcomes

Clinical Outcomes

Patient Satisfaction

Cost and Utilization

our children who are up-to-date on their immunizations; and (4) how we are
doing on our prenatal and well-child visits? Many of our payers will insist on
seeing these data.

Illustration 10.2   Basic Statistics for the Total Health Insurance Product (HMO, Managed Care, Medicaid HMO, Individual Company Plan, etc.)

Per Member per Month (PMPM); Statistics by Each Provider:

- Inpatient days PMPM
- Outpatient days PMPM
- Specialty services PMPM
- Total care PMPM
- Inpatient admissions per 1,000 members
- Inpatient average length of stay
- Paid by plan per inpatient admission
- Paid by plan per inpatient day
- Paid outpatient care claim
- Paid specialty care claim

Here is an example of a reporting form about patient satisfaction generated by a national healthcare marketing research corporation (see Illustration 10.3). The bar graph shows the results of three yearly surveys of member satisfaction for the Alpha Health Plan. Their satisfaction is improving, but tracks at below the average for all plans and is significantly below the best HMO in their market. Perceptions about access to specialty care are going down over time for Alpha Health Plan and are now significantly below the average of all HMOs and worse than the top HMO.

We're also thinking about generating another kind of report from information we can get now off our insurance information system. This physician report would give average information for all the members of the group and for the individual physician. It would show for Dr. Athens' patients, their average age, utilization by age, case severity, future risk, payments by diagnostic codes, and utilization over time compared to all the members in our HMO. A map would show the residence of patients coming to the group practice of Dr. Athens. A third report would list procedure codes and her charges to our health plan (see Illustration 10.4). If you look closely, you will see that these numbers are made up, but they give you a flavor of what they could look like.

Student: It looks like the doctors are being paid on a fee-for-service basis now rather than capitation. Can you lower costs that way?

Peter: Good question. There are several possibilities. Good physicians are ready to adjust their practice patterns to fit the partnership goals. We can change the payment methods and we would do this in cooperation with our platinum provider partners. With 90 practices, we can do cooperative experimental changes inviting some groups to change, measure the results,

Illustration 10.3   Alpha Health Plan—Health Plan Report of General Member Satisfaction, December 1995 (Total Sample N=384)

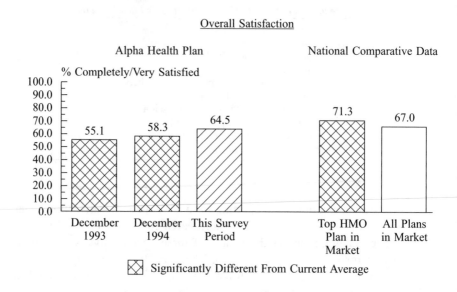

Overall Satisfaction

Alpha Health Plan   National Comparative Data

⬚ Significantly Different From Current Average

and then we all will watch to see what happens. The bottom line is that it is in all our interests to prosper and not go out of business.

However, our fee-for-service process is now the way our data are generated. We know who our enrollees are, where they live, and some basic demographics (age, sex, family size). We know the charges sent in by doctors, x-ray, labs, pharmacy, and hospitals linked to the patient and to the patient's primary doctor.

Student: What is a value compass?

Peter: Think of a regular compass. Patient satisfaction is measured in the northern direction, functional status (like average activities of daily living score) is to the west, costs per members per month to the south, and physiologic status to the east. Each of these is scored along each direction. The goal is to be farthest away from the center on all four directions. This form of presentation allows for comparisons with the previous level or with others.

I want one of your student teams to present to me what you think should be the core information for the physician's instrument panel. Be prepared to tell me how it will be collected, how it should be used, and how useful it will be for achieving our goal of excellent care at a reasonable and competitive price.

Illustration 10.4   A. R. Athens, M.D.: Procedure Codes Submitted to CCHP, 1/1/96–11/15/96

Description	Number	Total Charges	Average
Office/out PT visit (E&M) estab PT: moderate complexity, 25 min.	187	$12,903	$69
Office consultation new/estab PT: high complexity, 80 min.	55	$11,660	$212
Office/out PT visit (E&M) estab PT: low complexity, 15 min.	222	$11,100	$500
Inj., tendon sheath, ligament/trigger points/ganglion cyst	43	$3,080	$71
Arthrocentesis, aspiration and/or injection; major joint	25	$1,950	$78
Arthrocentesis, aspiration/inj.; small joint, bursa/ganglion	25	$1,550	$62
Office consultation new/estab PT: moderate complexity, 60 min.	7	$1,246	$178
Office consultation new/estab PT: low complexity, 40 min.	5	$780	$156
Arthrocentesis, aspiration and/or injection; intermed. joint	10	$670	$67
Office/out PT visit (E&M) estab PT: high complexity, 40 min.	5	$640	$128
Office consultation new/estab PT: low severity, 30 min.	5	$580	$116
Injection triamcinolone acetonide, per 10 mg	31	$465	$15
Office/out PT visit (E&M) estabablished PT: problem/minor, 10 min.	7	$287	$41
Immunization, active influenza virus vaccine	12	$180	$15
Administration of influenza virus vaccine	9	$90	$10
Incision & drainage of abscess; simple or single	1	$70	$70
Office/out PT visit (E&M) established PT: minimal, 5 min.	2	$68	$34
Methotrexate sodium, 50 mg	1	$23	$23
Injection, vitamin B\12 cyanocobalamin, up to 1000 mcg	2	$22	$11
		$47,364	

I have a task for the other student team. As you know, we can't just give out this information and expect it to be used. We are planning an ongoing continuing medical (and nursing) education program using the method of academic detailing. To start, when a group practice is ready to have a third individual and comparative practice data printout, one of our central office physicians and administrative staff will visit their plan to review their own information. We expect they will be interested in learning and improving in one or more of their care dimensions. We must be prepared to respond "just in time" to this perceived need with a package of learning material (articles, audiotapes, videotapes, special consultation, seminars, or whatever learning modality they prefer). If they want to improve patient satisfaction, we need to be ready with practical answers immediately.

Student: What is academic detailing?

Peter: It's the same idea as a drug company detail selling. The representative goes to the doctor's office to educate the physician about the benefits of his/her company's product. Academic detailing uses the same method, but sends out academic health center staff to provide education about good care practices.

I want the second student team to report back next week on the educational topics we need to have ready to go. Bring me a list and be prepared to explain the reasons for inclusion. You might even draft a full outline of a top-priority topic.

See you next week.

Short Case F

Working with Doctors at Suburban Community Hospital

Anthony R. Kovner

You are the board of Suburban Community Hospital. Your hospital has an excellent reputation in the community. In your target area, 60 percent of the area residents are admitted to Suburban Community and 40 percent are admitted to other nearby hospitals. Eighty-five percent of your admissions are from your target community. A number of large HMOs have been formed in your state, and large insurance companies have been developing point-of-service plans, involving the creation of provider networks. Your hospital, with other hospitals, has set up a large PPO and you are a participating provider in about 20 insurance plan networks.

Your CEO has informed you that the hospital's environment is forecasted to becoming increasingly problematic. Hospital utilization is expected to decrease substantially. Utilization of specialists is expected to decrease substantially as well. The trend is for large insurance companies to become increasingly selective regarding which hospitals and specialists participate in their provider networks. Many of the specialists on your medical staff are opposed to any plan in which hospital involvement would mean that all specialists could not participate. In neighboring states, primary care physicians are increasingly recruited by out-of-area hospitals into networks through which they hope to recruit specialty referrals. This has not yet happened in your community.

A prestigious outside consultant has recommended to the board that the hospital move proactively with its medical staff in a partnership arrangement in which some part of the medical staff would organize itself into a foundation, a staff model, or an equity model. The advantages of these models are (1) the strength of the tie between primary care physicians and the system; (2) alignment of physician provider interests to promote clinical efficiency; (3) positioning for the future ambulatory growth in healthcare; and (4) joint sharing of risk between the hospital and the physicians.

Your CEO agrees with the consultant concerning the long-range future and about what the hospital should attempt to bring about with its medical staff, but suggests that the time is not now right to make any major steps other than what the hospital is already engaged in—contracts as a participating provider with numerous insurance companies and formation of the PPO with other hospitals and their medical staff.

Case Questions:

- Should the hospital be doing anything else at this point to improve its future chances to maintain its present market standing?
- To what extent should the hospital and physicians be sharing risk, and what alternative relationships are acceptable to the board?
- Under what circumstances should the hospital attempt to move more quickly and more decisively toward cooperative contracting relationships with only selected members of the specialist medical staff?
- What data does the board require that it currently does not have in order to make better decisions in this area?

Short Case G

Complaining Doctor and Ambulatory Care

Anthony R. Kovner

You are the assistant director for ambulatory services. An attending physician complains, "The clerks are no good in this clinic, and neither is the director of nursing." What do you say to him? Assume that the physician is an important customer.

Later during the week, he is still not satisfied. Now **you** are the problem. What do you do now?

Short Case H

Doctors and the Capital Budget

Anthony R. Kovner

You are the hospital CEO. Doctors on the capital budget committee can't agree on which equipment to recommend for purchase and for how much. They are way over budget. What do you say to them?

Short Case I

Doctors and a New Medical Day Care Program for the Terminally Ill

Anthony R. Kovner

You are the hospital CEO. Medical staff is opposed to the hospital's providing needed day care to the terminally ill, which is forecasted to break even financially. They say this is not what the hospital is supposed to do, and that it will actually or potentially compete with their business. What do you say to them?

Short Case J

Average Length of Stay

Anthony R. Kovner

You are the hospital CEO. Two of the doctors consistently keep too many of their patients in the hospital longer than the average LOS for several DRGs. They say their patients are older and sicker and that they're practicing higher-quality medicine. What do you say to them?

Part **V**

Adaptation

Introduction

Adaptive capability involves organizational response to new conditions. Organizations must be innovative or proactive in manipulating their environment and responsive or reactive to the demands of constituent groups and actions of competitors. One indicator of adaptive capability is the presence of specialized units, such as a planning department, that are concerned specifically with and held accountable for the adapting function.

Planning as conducted by a special unit and by the manager is an important area of managerial contribution. The manager must constantly focus on how the organization is and should be adapting to justify the continued and increasing support of those who supply it with resources and who use or buy the organization's services.

Adapting decisions are based on information about the organization's mission, the nature of the services provided, the nature of the populations being served and to be served, the organization's competitive situation, and perceived obstacles to and opportunities for mission attainment and system maintenance.

Milio reminds us that organizations have limited problem-solving capacities, wish to avoid uncertainty by arranging negotiated environments, engage in problematic or biased searches for ways of adapting, act on the basis of limited knowledge, and select alternatives on the bases of past successes.[1]

Obviously, decisions to adapt can be the wrong ones relative to organizational goal attainment and system maintenance. Even if the decisions can be established, on hindsight, to have been technically appropriate, they might have been politically inappropriate. Managers may fail to develop a consensus on those directions toward which the organization should focus effort to minimize planning costs and to retain the energy and enthusiasms of key participants in the organization's ruling coalition. This is no small matter.

Changes in goal direction must often, of political necessity, be gradual or small. Otherwise, important participants who are opposed to such change will withhold their contributions. In a crisis, or at critical decision points involving major changes in organizational mission, such withdrawal may be an acceptable cost, provided that replacement participants are available who ·are willing and able to make the necessary contributions to organizational goal attainment and system maintenance.

The health services manager must anticipate the future in order to take advantage of emerging trends instead of opposing them, unless major organizational participants clearly understand and are willing to pay the price of such opposition.

In adapting to change, the manager must be constantly testing and interpreting the organization's environment to key submanager and interest groups, particularly medical staff officials. For goal attainment and system maintenance, organizations are often forced to make choices that involve closing or diminishing services and programs as well as investing in new or expanded services and facilities. Decisions that managers face in these cases are not usually made in relation to what else could be done with the dollars or to the time and political "chips" that must be spent on a particular management or regulatory initiative.

Circa 1997, mergers and acquisitions are sweeping the healthcare enterprise. Organizations that have been successful in the past are being forced to consider drastic changes in goals and strategy to be able to survive and grow in the future. Often this is only possible through partnerships and alliances or as a result of acquiring another organization or being merged into it. In the case of "The VNA of Cleveland" the CEO is faced with a set of choices involving new relationships with other health services organizations in Cleveland, some of which may be seen as threatening the core values upon which the VNA was founded and has thrived for many years.

Similarly, the CEO of the West Peoria Veterans Affairs Medical Center must decide how her center should relate to managed care and to other VA facilities in the region. A task force has recommended that 8,000 patients be initially enrolled in the VA Community Integrated Service Network. A marketing plan that includes the endorsement of veterans service organizations may be undertaken to enroll veterans not currently using VA, with the inclusion of new (and less ill) patients being seen as critical to success. Other options are recommended, and the CEO must examine critically the assumptions underlying the three options—and the realism of each option—in order to include opportunities for strategically aligning those interests necessary for implementation.

Case Questions

The VNA of Cleveland
- In which direction should the VNA go?
- How should the VNA board be brought along to agree with the change taken?
- How can staff morale be maintained in the face of this uncertainty?
- What are the issues that Mary Lou Stricklin must manage to succeed in implementing your recommendations?

In a State of Change
- What criteria would you use to choose among the three options selected in the case? What is your rationale for choosing these criteria?
- What are the advantages and disadvantages of each of the three options? How do the three options rate on each of the criteria you selected? What assumptions underlie your ratings?
- Which course of action do you recommend that Geraldine Patton pursue (assume that she must pursue an option)? What is the rationale behind your recommendation?
- How should Patton proceed in implementing your recommendations? What goals should she have and what strategies should she follow?
- What are the personal stakes involved for Patton in doing as you suggest? How can she maximize the upside potential and minimize the downside risks for her own career?

Notes

1. Nancy Milio, "Health Care Organizations and Innovation," in *Health Services Management: Readings and Commentary*, 2nd edition, edited by Anthony R. Kovner and Duncan Neuhauser, 448–464. (Chicago: Health Administration Press, 1983).

Selected Bibliography

Advisory Board Company, *The Grand Alliance: Vertical Integration Strategies for Physicians and Health Systems*. Washington, DC: Advisory Board Company, 1993.

Coddington, D. C., K. D. Moore, and E. A. Fischer. *Making Integrated Care Work*. Englewood, CO: Center for Research in Ambulatory Care Administration, 1996.

Griffith, J. R., V. K. Sahney, and R. A. Mohr. *Reengineering Health Care: Building on CQI*. Chicago: Health Administration Press, 1995.

Griffith, J. R. "Managing the Transition to Integrated Health Care Organizations." *Frontiers of Health Services Management.* 12, no. 4 (summer 1996): 4–50.

Zajac, E. J., and T. A. D'Aunno. "Managing Strategic Alliances" in *Essentials of Health Care Management,* edited by S. M. Shortell and A. D. Kaluzny, 328–364. Albany, NY: Delmar, 1997.

The Visiting Nurse Association of Cleveland

Duncan Neuhauser

Mary Lou Stricklin, MBA, MSN, is chief executive officer of the Visiting Nurse Association of Cleveland (VNA). The home care market continues to change rapidly. Competition, DRG payment, HMO growth, the rising burden of indigent care, hospital-based home care programs, hospice, large growth of demand for home care, and the explosion of specialized home care services all continue to affect the home care market. The national reform of healthcare is the hot topic of the day. These rapid changes have led to a series of corporate reorganizations, and Stricklin is contemplating the next corporate transformation.

1997 was the 95th anniversary of Cleveland's VNA. Throughout its history the VNA has employed professional nurses with home care experience to provide care to the residents of the greater Cleveland area, which now has a population of approximately 1.2 million people. The mission and value statements for the VNA are shown in Illustration 11.1.

1902–1980

The VNA remains as it began, an independent not-for-profit organization. Originally, it was supported largely by philanthropic contributions. In the early part of this century, Cleveland received a large immigrant population from Europe and later from the South. Its heavy industry base (steel, machine tools, automobiles) was and is cyclical in its level of activities, fluctuating from

Illustration 11.1   1995 Visiting Nurse Association of Cleveland: Mission, Vision and Values

---

Mission

To provide innovative, high-quality, and cost-effective community healthcare to all people by
- Delivering care that promotes health, independence, and dignity;
- Teaching people to care for themselves and each other; and
- Providing services to the poor as funds permit.

Charity Care

True to its mission, the VNA provided $1.6 million in charity care in 1995.

Vision
- To be the leader in innovative home care
- To be the standard for quality care
- To be the leader in community health planning and research

Values
- We value personal dignity, the importance of integrity, honesty and compassion.
- We are responsive to the needs of the community and our stakeholders.
- We value quality as a measurable outcome of emerging standards of performance.
- We value education and skill development of staff and clients.

---

high prosperity to slack times with layoffs and unemployment. The relative importance of this heavy industry declined in the late 1970s, resulting in a 10 percent population loss by 1985. Since then, the population has increased slightly and the economy has changed to services and regional distribution; Cleveland is the location of the corporate headquarters of 27 Fortune 500 corporations. As a result, there has been greater economic diversity and less cyclical unemployment. In the early 1990s, the economy has been doing a bit better than the national average.

Cleveland still has the highest per capita rate of philanthropic giving of any major city in the United States. The advent of Medicare and Medicaid in 1966 allowed for new revenue and expansion of the VNA. The original VNA board of trustees was largely composed of the wives of community leaders when one of the major board functions was to provide Christmas food baskets for needy patients. By the 1990s, the board was diverse by gender, ethnicity, and professional background.

1980: About the Only Game in Town

The 1980 organization chart of the VNA is shown in Illustration 11.2. The core professional staff consisted of full-time salaried generalist nurses who worked out of four district offices to cover Cleveland and adjacent townships. The center office included administrative staff to coordinate several part-time social workers and physical therapists. Calls requesting care were handled by the district offices where nurses were assigned to respond. The nurses themselves decided whether or not a patient was able to pay.

Home care aide services were also provided by the VNA under contract from another voluntary organization, the Center for Human Services. Special

Illustration 11.2   The Visiting Nurse Association of Cleveland Organization (1980)

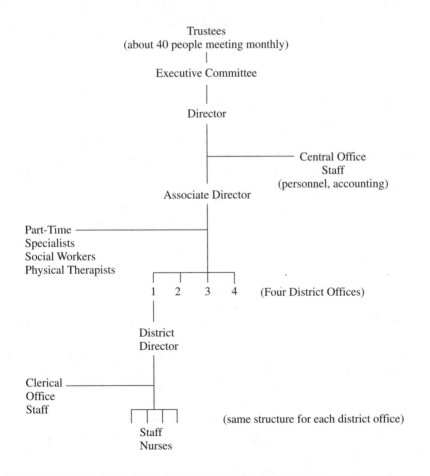

Reprinted with permission from the Visiting Nurse Associaton, Cleveland, Ohio.

contracts provided care for the elderly in several apartment complexes. All services were available during weekday working hours, and the agency was closed on weekends and holidays.

1982: Arrival of Competition

Ohio regulations made it easy to start a home care company, and over 300 were created. The joke went that if you had a telephone and knew a nurse, you could start a home care agency. If costs could be kept down and full-pay patients selected, home care could be profitable. By 1982, there was growing competition for paying home care patients. Others were content to let the VNA provide home care for those who could not pay. In 1984, VNA philanthropic gifts and endowment income yielded $190,000, plus United Way contributions of $540,000, out of a total of $5,000,000 in revenue. This allowed the VNA to provide care to all who requested it. However, the VNA needed mostly paying patients in order to survive.

This competitive situation led the VNA to ask for the first time the source of its patients, and how the choice of home care provider was made. It turned out that 82 percent of patients came by way of hospital discharge and, of these, most came from a dozen of the area's largest hospitals. Typically a nurse, social worker, or discharge planner made the decision within the hospital. The choice of provider depended primarily on agency reputation, the ease of making a referral, and agency name recall.

Instead of being a passive receiver of telephone requests for services, the VNA decided to assign a staff nurse as contact person for each major hospital in addition to regular nursing care activities. Brochures, calendars, and small magnetized VNA symbols were distributed to promote name recognition.

The VNA organized a centralized intake service with one recognizable telephone number as an important step in making referrals easier. At the VNA the belief was that one competitor was giving away transistor radios to hospital-based referrers. After some discussion, the VNA decided not to follow suit.

By 1983, DRG payments had drastically shortened patient stay and emptied hospital beds. Now the hospitals were encouraging earlier discharge combined with home care. Hospitals began actively looking for new revenue-generating ventures and hospital-based home care became popular.

By 1983, there was serious concern that the VNA's work would come to an end, as one hospital after another started its own home care program.

By 1984, a number of hospitals decided not to start their own programs, but rather to develop contracts with the VNA. The market again changed; no longer was it the individual nurse's or social worker's decision, but rather a hospital-based contract. One reason hospital contracting occurred was because hospital management was busy; the managers wanted to avoid a new program and save energy for higher-priority areas. By 1984, the VNA had contracts with eight hospitals, which accounted for about 35 percent of VNA's patients.

Early discharge drove the demand for increasingly complex home care requiring home care nurse specialists in intravenous (IV) management, pediatrics, mental health, hospice care, renal dialysis, and ostomy care, in addition to physical and occupational therapy and social work. This specialization and division of labor created economies of scale in home care. A small suburban hospital with paying patients and undifferentiated home care could prosper with small programs. Larger hospitals with more severely ill patients and high indigent care ratios found VNA contracting a better choice. Hospitals that started their own home care programs were unlikely to sell their program to nearby competing hospitals. Hospital contracts led to 24-hour service availability by the VNA rather than a 9-to-5 weekday organization. Hospitals wanted full-service agencies, so the VNA started homemaker services called "All for You." In response to these changes, the VNA reorganized in 1989.

1990–1995: Prosperity

The single not-for-profit [501(c)(3)] organization became four organizations and by 1995, six organizations. See Illustration 11.3.

The large group of trustees was divided into a smaller group of trustees with governance responsibility and a group of overseers—loyal supporters of the VNA with no line authority, but a right to advise and contribute.

In 1990, the VMA organizations numbered four:

- The bulk of the agencies' work was in VNA home care and within this, Medicare was the largest payor.
- "All For You" provided home aide assistance on a private basis (cleaning, food preparation, and personal hygienic care).
- VNA Enterprises was a small catch-all organization for receiving money for consulting and other services.
- VNA Lines provided IV solutions and other supplies needed in home care.

In the last several years, these four organizations have made surpluses; enough so that with fundraising, the VNA, in 1995, could move into a single new modern building in the center of the city near the expressway.

By clearly separating out the possible for-profit activities, the non-profit status of the whole organization could be preserved.

Illustration 11.3   Visiting Nurse Association of Cleveland (1994)

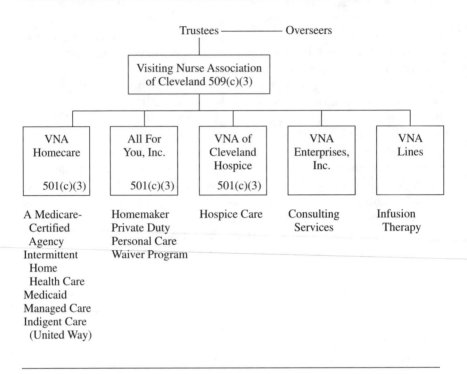

As of 1992, patients seen by the VNA were paid for as follows: Medicare, 86.6 percent; Medicaid, 5.21 percent; commercial insurance, 4.14 percent; Blue Cross, 1.82 percent; and other, 2.14 percent. Patient age range was 80 years and over, 30.5 percent; 60–79 years, 44 percent; 45–59 years, 10 percent; 10–44 years, 9.5 percent; and 0–9 years, 6 percent. Approximate overall revenues for 1993 were VNA, $22.5 million, "All For You," $2.9 million; and Hospice, $2.1 million.

Stricklin continued scanning the horizon to see what new changes were in store for healthcare. As of 1993, the projected future trends were summarized (see Illustration 11.4). She began to think of the VNA as a process of care and to conceive of the organization as a sequence of steps that all patients passed through (Illustration 11.5).

This pathway is driven by mission, vision, and values. Patients can be referred from nursing homes, physicians, hospitals, or affiliated networks such

Illustration 11.4   Projected Industry Trends, 1993

Home Care: Year 2000

Shift to Outpatient Care
Home care will be one of the fastest growing segments of the health care industry.
Home care patients will be significantly sicker and require more sophisticated care.
Home care will be an important element of pre- as well as post-acute care of a patient.

Accelerated Impact of Technology
The use of advanced medical technologies in home care will increase significantly.
New drug therapies will significantly change how patients are treated.
The use of computer, communication, and information technologies in home care will
    greatly expand.

Increased Managed Care Penetration
Managed home health care services will pervade.
Managed care organizations will have significant control over a patient's choice of provider.
Home health services will be carved out for national and regional contracting.
Accreditation, consistency, image, and brand name recognition will be important in com-
    peting for national/regional contracts.
Case management will play a key role in managed care.
Standard treatment protocols will cover most care.

Demand for Quality/Outcome Measures
Employers and payers will demand quality and outcome measures.
Meaningful quality and outcome measures for home care will be developed.
Quality and outcome measures will be used to select home care providers.

Emphasis on Wellness, Prevention, and a Healthy Lifestyle
Employers/payers will cost-justify wellness programs.
Wellness, prevention, and a healthy lifestyle will be emphasized.
Individuals will be interested and actively involved in their own care.

More Enlightened Public Policy
All citizens will be guaranteed universal access to basic health care benefits.
Reimbursement for health care services will be fair and equitable.
A "two-tier" health care delivery status will be our primary goal.

Emergence of Regional Health Care Delivery Systems
Integrated, health care delivery systems offering a full continuum of care will dominate
    local markets.
Collaboration and networking of health care organizations will be prevalent.
"Free-Standing" health care organizations will be rare.

Reprinted with permission from the Visiting Nurse Association, Cleveland, Ohio.

as the Comprehensive Care Network (CCN) of several home care agencies' coordinating services. Communications in use include voice mail, fax, pagers, e-mail, and cellular phones. Risk adjusters are used to predict how patients will respond to care so that care plans (Maps to Wellness) can be modified.

A national effort is underway among visiting nurse associations to develop a computerized patient information and management system. This is to be linked to an automated system to record services provided. Applied research and development is essential for advancing such systems of care.

In 1995, the Cleveland VNA provided 342,947 visits for 11,899 patients, 77.6 percent paid by Medicare. Hospice served 733 patients and "All For You" provided 207,937 hours of service to 375 patients.

Major innovative services are described in Illustration 11.6. Quality is supported by an ethics advisory committee, a professional advisory committee, systematic staff evaluation of new technologies, the development of performance report cards for payors, patient satisfaction surveys, and an active CQI program: all of this with the ultimate goal of improving the health of the community.

1997: The Firestorm of Change in Healthcare

By now the 40 hospitals in the greater Cleveland area have grouped themselves into four fiercely competing systems of care: two are parts of a national for-profit system and two are local non-profit groups. Two of these groups have their own home care programs and tend to refer in-house. Mary Lou Stricklin is faced with a new set of choices:

Illustration 11.5   1995: The VNA Organization as a Process

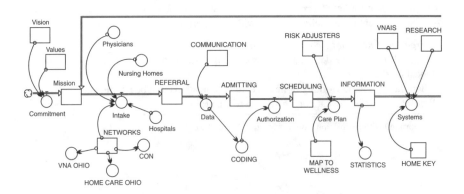

Option 1. Stay independent and hope that excellence will be recognized, working in partnership with some of these systems. The problem with this strategy is that the VNA could be left out in the cold.

Option 2. Several not-for-profit hospitals in town have sold out to for-profit systems. The money from the sale is turned into an endowed non-profit foundation and the hospital is run as a business. The VNA could do this, combining its endowment and the income from sale to create a home care foundation addressed to the goals the VNA has held since it started.

Option 3. The VNA could join with a nursing home chain in a merger, betting that elder long-term care will evolve into a managed care system with the aim of keeping people out of nursing homes with home care support.

In which direction should the VNA go? How should the VNA board be brought along to agree with the change taken? How can staff morale be maintained in the face of this uncertainty?

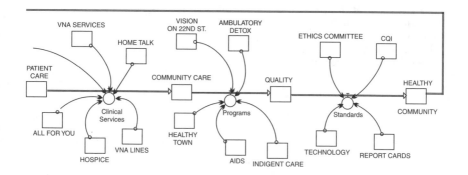

Illustration 11.6   Visiting Nurse Association of Cleveland (1995)

Innovations

Home Talk™
Through a joint venture with Telepractice in the fall of 1995, VNA introduced Home Talk™, a free telephone service for patients that improves access to their VNA clinician. Patients may choose from several options, including an on-line library with recorded health information. Home Talk™ supports the clinician's assessment of a patient's health status resulting in fewer readmissions to the hospital and unnecessary trips to the emergency room.

Ambulatory Detoxification Services
The VNA of Cleveland, MetroHealth, and Alcoholism Services of Cleveland are collaborating on an 18-month demonstration project to provide ambulatory detoxification services and chemical dependency care in home and community settings. This project is funded by a grant from the Cleveland Foundation.

Healthy Town
This program provides health promotion and disease prevention services to lower-income senior citizens and families with children at University Settlement and Collinwood Community Services Center, member organizations of the Neighborhood Centers Association. Funding is provided by the CAVS Charities and the Cleveland Foundation.

HIV/AIDS Mental Health
Through a grant from the AIDS Funding Collaborative, the VNA and the Free Clinic are collaborating to bring nursing care, social work, and consultative services to patients.

KID Connection
KID Connection nurses offer educational programs and consultation services for child care providers. These services help day care staff deliver high-quality care and meet state licensing requirements.

Vision on 22nd Street
To prepare students for community-based nursing, the VNA and Cleveland State University Department of Nursing formed an education-service partnership. A committee of community healthcare experts from both institutions developed new nursing curricula and began offering classes last fall. The program will educate over 200 nursing students within the next few years. Vision on 22nd Street is partially funded by the Cleveland Foundation.

Clozaril Management
Selected patients of the Mental Health program are participating in VNA's collaborative research study, funded by Sandoz Pharmaceuticals, to evaluate the effectiveness of Clozaril, and to implement the program in other areas of the country.

Camp TLC
VNA Hospice's Bereavement Camp TLC, Together Love Continues, is an annual day-long program helping children and family members who have lost a loved one to cope with their grief. The camp is underwritten by the Bicknell Fund.

In a State of Change: Veterans Affairs and HMOs

J. J. Donellan, A. R. Kovner, C. A. Milbrandt, J. Oliveri, B. L. Bell, D. Anderson, and P. J. O'Neil

The state of West Peoria leads the nation in healthcare reform. In each of the past three legislative sessions comprehensive healthcare reform laws have been passed. The legislation has brought about the following:

- The small employer insurance market has been restructured to enable more citizens to acquire health insurance coverage. Within two years all employers with more than 50 employees will be required to offer and subsidize coverage for employees and their dependents.

- A state-funded health insurance program has been created to cover those citizens unable to obtain private insurance and who do not qualify for other government health programs. This program has been in effect for the past year and is offered on a sliding fee basis.

- In three years universal coverage for West Peoria will be implemented. At that time all West Peorians will be required by law to acquire a minimum "basic benefit" package.

With the advent of universal coverage most health providers will organize into integrated service networks (ISNs). Reimbursement rates for providers not participating in an ISN will be regulated by a state-run all-payor system (a modified fee-for-service system) that will severely restrict reimbursement.

ISNs will be licensed by the state and will be required to provide, at a minimum, the basic benefit package prescribed by law to anyone wishing to enroll.

Community ISNs (CISNs), a smaller version of an ISN, may begin enrolling patients immediately. Both ISNs and CISNs are required to make primary care services available within 30 miles of an enrollee's home. Secondary and tertiary services (with the exception of highly specialized services such as transplants, open heart surgery, and neurosurgery) must be available within 60 miles of an enrollee's home. Growth in ISN/CISN premium rates will be state regulated, and "report cards" comparing ISN and CISN performance on factors such as cost, quality, and customer satisfaction will be issued annually by the state.

HMOs and managed care plans have been developing in West Peoria since the 1950s. The market is dominated by managed care, with two-thirds of the state's 8 million citizens enrolled in some form of managed care plan. Three HMOs now dominate the managed care market, covering 80 percent of the state's managed care enrollees.

Geraldine Patton was recently appointed director of the Dwight D. Eisenhower VA Medical Center in Peoria City (Peoria City VAMC). Patton was assigned to Peoria City by VA Central Office (VACO) for the specific purpose of developing and implementing a transition plan that will ensure VA's success in West Peoria's reformed healthcare market.

Peoria City VAMC is the largest of three VA medical centers in the state and is geographically located near the center of the state. The facility is five years old and is considered by many to be among the finest and most modern of the 170 VA medical centers nationwide. It currently consists of a 500-bed acute care hospital with medical, surgical, rehabilitation medicine, and psychiatric beds, and a 100-bed nursing home. It is a major teaching affiliate of the University of West Peoria Medical School. With the exception of transplantation services, all primary, secondary, and tertiary healthcare services are available at the facility or through a sharing agreement with the university. These include a newly opened women veterans health program and a nationally renowned prosthetic and rehabilitation center. The Medical Center also manages a satellite outpatient clinic located 50 miles to the south of Peoria City. The veteran population of the state of West Peoria is 520,000. Peoria City VAMC treated 38,000 individual veteran patient cases during the past year.

Some management improvements are necessary at Peoria City VAMC. Length of stay for both medicine and surgery is three to five days longer than that found in comparable non-VA community and teaching hospitals. Waiting times for next available appointments are more than 30 days in many of the specialty clinics, and pressure to reduce overall government employment has forced staffing reductions in virtually all departments. A primary care program has recently been instituted, with approximately 25 percent of all outpatients enrolled in this program. Primary care has had a positive effect. Overall, waiting times for next clinic appointments have been reduced, and the satisfaction of patients served by a primary care provider has improved.

Two other VA medical centers are also located in West Peoria. The Lakeland VAMC is located 125 miles to the north of Peoria City, close to the state's northern border. This 150-bed facility offers primary and secondary health services to approximately 12,000 veterans and operates a specialized spinal cord injury program. The Leesville VAMC, located 90 miles to the southeast of Peoria City, operates a 350-bed acute and chronic care psychiatric hospital and a 250-bed nursing home. The hospital specializes in the care of chronic psychiatric patients, with specialized programs of excellence in substance abuse and post-traumatic stress. The nursing home operates at full capacity with a waiting list for admission. A small clinic at Leesville offers primary care services to approximately 10,000 veterans on an outpatient basis. Both the Lakeland and Leesville facilities were built in the 1930s; although some modernization has been done, they are both in need of considerable plant improvements. All three West Peoria VA medical centers are part of a referral network that also includes two VA medical centers in neighboring East Peoria, and one in the state of Tremont, located to the south of West Peoria.

Geraldine Patton appointed a task force from the Peoria City VAMC to analyze the current situation and present an action plan. The task force consisted of the chief of staff, Dr. Urban Grant (Chairperson), several medical staff leaders, the associate dean for clinical programs at the University of West Peoria Medical School, the chief of medical administration and fiscal services, and leaders of three different veterans service organizations in the immediate community. Dr. Grant's task force reached consensus on establishing a VA-sponsored CISN based at Peoria City VAMC, with future plans to expand to a statewide ISN in conjunction with the Lakeland and Leesville VAMCs. The report included a financial analysis projecting that a benefit package providing comprehensive coverage meeting state criteria would cost $1,500 per enrollee under age 65, and $5,200 per enrollee age 65 and over (exclusive of supplemental services such as long-term care). For enrolled veterans not living near existing facilities, primary care and emergency services could be offered close to their home by shifting resources to set up multiple community clinics and by establishing contracts with community hospitals and providers.

The task force recommended that 8,000 patients be initially enrolled in the VA CISN; 4,000 should come from Peoria City VAMC's existing patient population, and an additional 4,000 new enrollees should be sought. A marketing plan that included the endorsement of veterans service organizations would be undertaken to enroll veterans not currently using VA. The inclusion of new (and less ill) patients was seen as critical to success; the existing patient base of Peoria City VAMC was disproportionately skewed toward patients with multiple and chronic medical conditions.

The task force also recommended that Peoria City VAMC contract with MetroPru, a large health insurer in West Peoria, to do the actuarial work, to manage enrollment, billings, and collections, and to ensure that equivalent insurance options would be made available as a package to the dependents of veterans who chose to enroll. The cost of contracting with MetroPru to manage the plan was not factored into the report. The task force felt confident that the plan would be competitive in that it would offer health benefits to veterans not customarily available in other CISN/ISN packages (i.e., low-cost prescriptions and broad coverage for psychiatric benefits). Some legislative relief would be necessary, most especially from total employment restrictions. An additional funding stream would also be needed to meet the increased number of patients served. This could be accomplished either by an increase in funding to Peoria City VAMC by VACO based on new enrollment, or through legislative relief permitting Peoria City VAMC to retain insurance collections.

Mrs. Patton discussed the task force recommentations with the directors of the Lakeland and Leesville VAMCs at a network meeting. They were less than enthusiastic. While Peoria City VAMC was well capitalized, the Lakeland and Leesville facilities simply did not have the physical plant and access to staff necessary to compete in the market. They questioned the urgency of such a drastic action, pointing out that many patients already elected to receive care by VA despite having other health insurance, including Medicare. In their opinion, the state reform agenda might in fact create a greater demand for VA care, noting that ISNs would likely exclude coverage of service-connected illness or injury, and offer only very limited psychiatric and long-term care benefits.

They suggested that rather than form an ISN or CISN, the medical centers specifically identify clinical areas of expertise and cost efficiency and aggressively market those services to health insurers. The insurers could purchase these services from VA for eligible veterans enrolled in their plans. They argued that those treatment areas not covered by the required "basic benefit" package where VA had specific expertise, such as prosthetic programs, long-term care, geriatric care, acute and chronic psychiatry, substance abuse, and PTSD, would become a critical "safety net" for veterans, and an essential ingredient of the state program. Finally, they noted that their strategy would require little action in terms of redirecting resources and facility missions.

Ms. Patton is familiar with another option not yet presented, but one that she was involved in negotiating with the state of Columbia during her last assignment. Rather than trying to initially compete in the market as an insurer, VA could negotiate an arrangement directly with the state, whereby state payments and subsidies would be waived for any care provided to non-service-connected veterans who met VA criteria for mandatory treatment and who elected to receive their care at a VA facility. Through such an arrangement, low-income non-service-connected veterans eligible for state-funded health insurance could receive their care by VA under the auspices of the state plan but at no cost to the state. As category "A" patients, their care would be covered by federal appropriations rather than state payment. This was seen as a win-win arrangement in Columbia. VA gained experience as a provider and administrator of a managed care plan in the early stages of state reform; the state realized savings by avoiding any costs associated with the care of low-income veterans receiving VA care.

Acknowledgments

The authors wish to thank Gary DeGasta, Brian Heckert, and Malcolm Randall for their ideas and suggestions, and for their critical review of the case.

Part **VI**

Accountability

Introduction

Accumulating evidence suggests a significant misallocation of medical care resources relative to improving the health of the American people. At a time when the nutrition, health, and training of low-income groups are neglected, there are too many hospital beds, too much surgery, too many lab tests, and too many medical specialists practicing in high-income areas. Who is accountable? Who is responsible? What—to the manager—are the consequences of pursuing organizational accountability?

When patients complain, how is the manager to know whether or not their complaints are justified? When he knows their complaints *are* justified, what can he do to resolve them satisfactorily? It *costs* patients in time to complain, and their expectations concerning appropriate remediation may be low. To what extent should the manager lower patient costs in complaining or help develop and share organizational goals that will limit and focus patient and consumer expectations?

Managers are paid to help the organization attain goals and to obtain a level of resources and productivity necessary for system maintenance. The various stakeholders in health services organizations include trustees, managers, physicians, other professionals, nonprofessionals, patients, and payors. Vendors and volunteers also have a stake in organizational performance. The authors maintain that accountability is limited unless there is some mutual agreement among stakeholders on goals, satisfactory ways to measure goals attainment, and a satisfactory way of altering organizational goals.

The process of goal definition, goal sharing, and goal measuring is a costly one. Conflict among key stakeholders will escalate to the extent that important disagreement is present, affecting or potentially affecting a major shift in resources allocation. In the process of agreeing on goals, certain members of the ruling coalition may exit or attempt to force out other members.

The alternative to formal accountability is mutual adjustment. Rather than establishing goals, interest groups confront each decision on its merits and its effect on them. Should the organization purchase or lease a CT scanner, provide services or not to the chronically ill, or purchase or lease new computer services? If any significant minority of the ruling coalition objects to a new policy direction, then such a direction will be vetoed until consensus can be achieved. This prevents major mistakes and time wasted on resolving conflict, in reaching agreement on measurement, and in lengthy discussions with various groups concerning whom the organization serves and should serve and about which services to expand, dilute, initiate, or discontinue.

Obviously, if services are being provided satisfactorily, there is no reason for managerial involvement. This is seldom the case, however, because of scarce resources and high patient expectations. If managers do not systematically attempt to assure quality and adequate service and access, they will not occur. To the extent that managers have such organizational responsibilities and to the extent that physicians and nurses are accountable to a chief executive officer, managers should involve themselves directly with patient care.

Of course, in some health services organizations physicians and nurses are formally accountable for patient care only to their peers and to patients. Often, however, the manager sees something wrong or patients complain to her. The manager can respond directly to certain problems, such as uncleanliness, lack of information systems, or employees in the emergency room who don't speak the language of many patients. Other problems, such as physician or nurse rudeness, malpractice, and lack of regular physician visits to patients, can be referred to departmental chiefs or nursing administration. The manager can communicate with patients by survey or interview to find out how they perceive services and how services can be improved.

As a rule, patients do not wish to get involved with organizational functioning. They want things to run smoothly. Patients expect to be treated equitably compared to other patients. They expect not to be harmed by doctors, nurses, and others. Many feel their time is valuable. Patients want to be relieved of pain. They expect appropriate access to care, and some want explanations of their problems and the treatment options open to them with probable related costs and benefits. Patients wish to be treated with dignity and with respect for their privacy, except when critically ill. They wish to pay a fair price. How patients feel about the care they receive varies by factors relating to demographic characteristics, provider characteristics, and services offered.

Managers expect patients to continue using the facility for services, to complain if they feel they are not properly treated, to make decisions about their own healthcare, to expect only the possible from providers (certain illnesses are not curable, sufficient staff are not always available), to respect the rights of other patients and providers, and to respect the facility's equipment and supplies.

These seem like reasonable expectations, of both patients and managers. Why then don't people in health services organizations behave as patients expect, and vice versa? First there is the lack of formal accountability of physicians, for reasons discussed in the section on physician integration. Related is the lack of dependence by some physicians for income on the organization within which they work or on particular patients whom they serve. Also related is the lack of competition among physicians as reflected in the lack of price and service information for consumers. A consumer does not usually consider choice of hospital in choosing a physician, yet the choices are usually confined because most physicians admit primarily, if not almost exclusively, to one hospital. Inpatients do not usually complain because they are not prepared to leave the hospital if dissatisfied and must remain dependent for service on those about whose services they would be complaining. Many persons do not want to make decisions about their care but rather to trust in the physician. When physicians are reimbursed largely on their costs, there is often insufficient incentive to remain efficient. When physicians are paid by the service rather than by the patient, there is an incentive to provide more services rather than to spend more time with each patient. When physicians are paid on salary or by the patient, there is a tendency to see fewer patients. Physicians and patients are human beings, as are managers, and all have their own failings and strengths.

When service breaks down, what options are open to patients and consumers? Patients may take or threaten to take their business elsewhere. They may complain, in the case of a physician, to a department chief, a manager, or a member of the board of trustees. They may form patient organizations (as in chronic care facilities) to advocate for their rights. Patients can sue to recover costs from a provider's malpractice. Patients can lead healthier lives so they are less dependent on the healthcare system; they can raise their tolerance for pain and discomfort. Consumers can control the facility by obtaining positions on governing boards and reporting back to their constituencies. Government regulatory agencies, national accrediting agencies, and large purchasers can represent consumers and patients in holding providers accountable for meeting minimally adequate standards of care.

Managers can undertake marketing studies to find out what patients and consumers like and do not like about the organization's services. Managers can set up special organizational units to advocate for patients, such as patient relations coordinators, patient care committees, or advisory committees. Work can be reorganized so that fewer people provide more services for each patient, as in primary nursing. Organizational routines can be reevaluated periodically in terms of patient outcome or inconvenience as well as provider convenience. Special units or committees can be organized for assuring quality of care. The manager can tour the facility regularly, talk with staff and patients, and observe how services can be improved and made more convenient. The manager can lower the costs of patient complaining by establishing a hotline. The manager can analyze complaints, their resolution, and follow-up, and can talk to complainants personally. The manager can let patients know what they are likely to expect when they come for services and what behavior is expected from them.

To whom is the healthcare organization accountable? How is it accountable? How can its level of performance be ascertained by those who wish to hold it accountable or by those who are concerned with demonstrating that it is accountable? We have referred previously to the various stakeholders or participants who have an interest in the performance of a health services organization. The manager can report regularly to constituent groups as to performance, plans, and problems. Members of such constituencies can be included on policymaking and advisory committees. Management information systems can be developed to gain access to data needed for planning and evaluating services; data would include information on the population served, the population using various services, quantities of service provided, cost of service provided, quality of service provided, and patient satisfaction. Summaries of reports of regulators and accreditors can be shared with participants and stakeholders. Organizational goals and goal performance can be analyzed as can information relating to system maintenance concerns such as trends in turnover, overtime and absenteeism, fund-raising, profit and loss, and new capital equipment. The process of decision making itself can be examined and improved either as a process given certain ends, or by including new stakeholders who are affected significantly by policy decisions of the organization or who can affect them. By making itself accountable, the organization incurs substantial costs in terms of time of key trustees and owners, physicians, and managers; monies spent on information systems; and conflicts raised about present and future direction. But the organization may also reap substantial benefits by making plans more acceptable to key stakeholders and therefore more feasible to implement, in gained commitment from key providers of needed services to the organization, and in sharper focusing of the organization's mission so that goal attainment is more easily obtained and justified to stakeholders and participants.

The two long cases presented in this section deal with accountability from different perspectives. "A Personal Memorandum on Hospital Experience" provides the patient's point of view, and "Whose Hospital?" provides the manager's. The short cases deal with managerial conflicts of interest and the management of diversity.

Case Questions

Personal Memorandum on Hospital Experience

- How do you feel about the level of patient care given in this medical center? How do you think the patients feel? The doctors? The managers?
- What are some of the problems with patient care in the hospital? What are the most important problems that you can do something about?
- What are the causes of the problems?
- As the hospital CEO, what would you do if you had received this memorandum?
- How would you have solved the problems to which the author refers?
- What organizational factors would constrain implementation of your solutions?
- How would you overcome these constraints?

Whose Hospital?

- How do you feel about what happened to Wherry?
- Do you feel the board was justified in acting as it did?
- What could Wherry have done or not done to prevent being fired? What could the board have done? What should the medical board have done?
- Should Wherry have resigned as the board wished him to?
- Whose hospital is it? What are the consequences for consumers, patients, managers, physicians, and trustees?

Selected Bibliography

Cleary, P. D., et al. "Patients Evaluate Their Care: A National Survey." *Health Affairs* 10 (winter 1991): 254–267.

Council on Ethical and Judicial Affairs, American Medical Association. "Ethical Issues in Managed Care." *Journal of the American Medical Association*. 273, no. 4 (25 January 1995): 330–336.

Griffith, J. R. *The Moral Challenges of Health Care Management*. Chicago: Health Administration Press, 1993.

Leebov, W., and G. Scott. *Service Quality Improvement: The Customer Satisfaction Strategy for Health Care*. Chicago: American Hospital Publishing, 1993.

Strasser, S., and R. M. Davis. *Measuring Patient Satisfaction for Improved Patient Services*. Chicago: Health Administration Press, 1991.

Thomasma, D. C. "Promise-Keeping: An Institutional Ethos for Healthcare Today." *Frontiers of Health Services Management* 13, no. 2 (winter 1996): 5–34.

A Personal Memorandum on Hospital Experience

Elias S. Cohen

Recently, I spent some seventeen days in a hospital of very fine repute, indeed, one of the finest medical centers of the East. While there I underwent two surgical assaults on my system and had sufficient time to do some observing from a patient's point of view.

I occupied a semiprivate room and enjoyed the company of one roommate during my entire stay. My roommate was a man seventy-two years of age, in the hospital receiving treatment for metastatic carcinoma of the esophagus. While he had been in this country for some thirty years, his command of the English language was not good; indeed, he was most comfortable speaking in his native German. He was fully ambulatory and received cobalt therapy daily. His esophagus was somewhat obstructed so that it was necessary for him to subsist on a bland and liquid diet.

In contrast to my own situation he was very much alone. His wife had passed away four months earlier. They had been childless. A dog which they had had for sixteen years had died about five or six months before his wife passed away. He had a sister in New York, a brother in Florida, and a brother in Australia. His sister visited him once a week, and he received mail at least every other day.

This, then, was the environment in which I resided for some seventeen days recovering from two operations performed a week apart. These observations are in no way meant to suggest that the situations I encountered were the case in all situations, or were necessarily typical throughout this one hospital. I was stimulated, however, by this experience to reflect upon the meaning of hospital care for some patients and the impact of various aspects of hospital operation on the consumer of hospital service.

On Admissions

I had been told that I was to be at the hospital at 10:30 a.m. in order to be admitted for hospitalization. I arrived shortly before that only to learn that hospital admissions were scheduled for 11:00 a.m. I was asked to have a seat in a very pleasant lounge, and I thereupon waited for about an hour before I was called by an admitting clerk. The admitting clerk took the usual information and received the customary authorizations for treatment, waivers, etc. She was most pleasant and told me that it would probably be some time before the room would be ready. In this case she suggested that I might want to go down to the snack bar and have a cup of coffee and otherwise relax. I took her advice, and about forty-five minutes or an hour later my name was called and I was escorted to my room.

Upon arriving at the room I found that the bed was not made, the floor was not swept; indeed, it was visibly dirty. I was told I might want to go up to the lounge and wait, which I did. Subsequently I returned to the room and found the bed had been made. The floor was still dirty. I asked the nurse if I should change into pajamas and was told to do so. At no point did anyone tell me what the routine might be that first day and if I had any anxieties about my hospital admission. There appeared to be no awareness of this by anyone on the floor. It would seem to me that there are a number of patients who arrive at their hospital room quite anxious about what is going to happen, perhaps somewhat awed and afraid of this new environment, who could benefit substantially by having a nurse come in, introduce himself, and explain what the general routine for that particular day might be, including the request for specimens, the taking of blood, a visit by the physician at some particular hour if they know it, some explanation about meal service, and some offer to explain whatever the patient might want. It may be thought that the very nice brochure that the hospital had prepared was sufficient. However, I would venture that the personal contact, and whatever suggestion of reassurance might be offered, would be helpful to many patients.

On Design

I was struck by the severe inadequacies of design in this facility. The room, which had been designed for two beds, as manifested by the two fixtures for piped-in oxygen, the recessed cubicle curtain rods, and the two call bells, was decidedly undersized. I learned this, to my discomfort, upon my return from surgery on two occasions when an inordinate amount of jockeying and bumping of the surgical litter took place in order to bring the litter next to the bed. In order to make room for the litter the following pieces of furniture had to be moved: my roommate's bed, my bed, my roommate's bedside table, and one of the two easy chairs in the room. The only pieces of furniture in the room which were *not* moved were the other easy chair and the two bedside cabinets.

Apart from this, I would point out that my bed was generally no more than a foot and a half away from my roommate's bed. The other side of my bed was about three to four feet away from the adjacent wall. My bed was the one located closest to the door. If I, or a guest, were sitting in the easy chair located at the foot of my bed, it was impossible for anyone to pass between the person sitting in the easy chair and the foot of my bed without either bumping my bed or asking the individual to move his chair.

While the hospital has very liberal visiting hours, it would have been impossible for my roommate and me to have had more than one visitor at a time.

These deficiencies in room size are all the more surprising when one considers that this building was constructed within the last five years.

It was equally surprising to find the toilet fixtures in the bathroom without any kind of adjacent hand rails. Indeed, there were no hand rails of any kind in the corridors or any place else that I was able to observe.

The lounge on this floor, which is the only place where a person can go if he wants to walk outside of his room, was located at an extreme end of the floor. Its design and furniture layout were such that it was virtually impossible for two or three people to gather in a knot to talk. It is a large room with some couches and chairs placed around the periphery with a television set at one end. There is nothing there to invite three or four ambulatory patients to sit in a small group, or for a patient who may have a couple of visitors to go to the lounge and sit in a way that the three people might face each other. The lounge is windowless and dimly lighted. It seemed, in all respects, a place that would tend to deaden socialization or the opportunity for patients to converse together. Indeed, as some of my comments below will indicate, there were many things in this hospital that seemed to conspire to keep patients very much alone.

For the lonely patient, and particularly the elderly patient who may be facing a terminal illness or an illness that threatens to change his lifestyle, loneliness can be a very destructive force. With increasing numbers of elderly making use of our hospitals I would venture the suggestion that just as we encourage nursing homes to take into account the social needs of their patients, so we must encourage our hospitals to recognize the social needs of their patients.

On Medical Surveillance

I could not help but be enormously impressed with the medical surveillance extended to me and to my roommate. Our physicians and the residents assigned to us were in to check with us no less than twice a day and more typically three and four times a day. The residents gave every appearance of competence, of concern, and of conscientious attention. They were alert and were careful to explain what they were about to do, what it was that was going to happen to us, etc. They were ready to answer questions.

I must comment, however, on one instance concerning my roommate. In the course of making the diagnosis of cancer of the esophagus it was necessary to insert an instrument into his esophagus in order to secure a sample of tissue. He told me if he had to undergo it again he would prefer to die.

One day when his physician was inquiring about how he was eating and whether the food was adequate and whether he was able to swallow, he complained that he was having difficulty. His physician explained that the cobalt treatments might tend to inflame the esophagus somewhat, cause swelling, and thereby make swallowing a difficult procedure. However, if it became too difficult, the physician went on to explain, it would be a small thing to insert a plastic tube through which he could be fed. It was evident, almost at that moment, that my roommate equated the insertion of this plastic feeding tube with the examination he had undergone earlier. He had no opportunity then and there, and he was not quick enough, because of his language problem, to complain about this possibility. All through that day the man worried himself almost into a great state of anxiety. Finally, in the evening he could bear it no more and he asked the nurse to call a physician. When the physician came, one of the residents, he told the resident that he would not permit the insertion of a plastic tube. The resident said, "I thought you didn't understand it when your doctor told you about it," and he then went on in a very calm, kind, and humane manner to explain to my roommate that this would be a very simple and painless procedure that had no relationship to the examination he had undergone earlier. This came as a great relief to my roommate, but he had spent a day torturing himself over the chance and, indeed, innocent remark of his physician.

The point here is that physicians must take great care, particularly with the elderly, the uninformed, and with those who perhaps have language difficulties, to explain in some detail what it is they might do, how much pain may be involved, how difficult the situation is, etc.

Perhaps the thing that is worse even than pain in a hospital is not knowing. It is the not knowing when something is going to happen, or the not knowing what is going to happen, how much it will hurt, how long it will hurt, what has been done to you, why your body is or isn't reacting in a certain way, what the chances are that things will get better or not get better, how serious some development is, what medication is supposed to do, etc., that is difficult to endure.

On Nursing Service

Perhaps the most noteworthy comment I can make on the nursing service is its variability in the face of extraordinarily conscientious supervision, hard work, dedication, and attentiveness to duty. The level of discipline appeared high—and I use the word discipline in the sense of adherence to routines, safeguarding the issuance and handling of medications, recordkeeping, shift-to-shift reporting on each and every patient, etc.

1. The numbers of staff seemed to be adequate but certainly not excessive.
2. All staff were uniformly pleasant, jovial, and apparently interested.
3. The nursing assistants did their work well and with dispatch.
4. Nurses receiving additional training were very good.

Thus, it is so surprising in retrospect the neglect with which I was treated on my return from surgery the first time. I was brought back from the recovery room about 1:30 p.m. From that time until 9:15 the following morning, with the single exception of responses of nurses to give me painkilling shots, I received no attention from any nurse. Despite the fact that the room was beastly hot and I and my wife had complained about the heat, despite the fact that I was drenched most of the time with perspiration, particularly through the night during which I endured the discomforts of a Foley catheter, nobody washed my face or offered a cool washcloth, nobody suggested or advised me that I might have a pain shot sooner than I had requested it. Nobody, in fact, even inquired as to whether there was anything they could do to make me more comfortable. No one came in to straighten a sheet. No one offered to change the position of my legs although it was difficult, if not impossible, for me to move them without some help.

Early in the evening of the day on which I was first operated on, I was visited by a member of my staff who is a registered nurse. In talking with me, she observed that the IV fluid was infiltrating. She brought this to the attention of an orderly, who recognized the situation for what it was immediately, and advised the nurses who subsequently called a physician to reinsert the IV. It appeared this had been infiltrating for some time. Apparently the IV had not been adequately checked.

During that first afternoon and night following surgery I think I had more attention and time from physicians than I did from nurses. On that day and the day or two following, but at no other time during the rest of my seventeen days of hospital stay, I found the response to the call button singularly bad. It was not uncommon to wait twenty minutes or more for someone even to come over the enunciator system to ask what it was I wanted. In that first day or two following surgery it was not uncommon to wait an additional fifteen minutes or so after I had made my wants known. I think this bothered me most when I asked for some relief from pain. It wasn't the waiting so much as the feeling that perhaps they were insensitive. I am sure that this is not correct. It would have made waiting so much easier if someone had answered the enunciator and had said, "It's going to take us ten or fifteen minutes to get to you. We're in the midst of trying to give somebody a treatment," "We're in the midst of preparing our medications," or, "Everybody is out in the rooms trying to serve the patients," or something of that sort. At least I would have known that they were trying, which I am sure they were.

As it turned out, on the second day after surgery I had a chance encounter with the field representative from the State Department of Public Welfare, which supervises and approves the hospital. She was making rounds with a representative from the administrator's office and she encountered me quite by accident. I explained to her what I had found at the hospital and what my experience had been. Following that encounter the nursing service visibly improved. I don't say this to suggest that there was a connection. Frankly, I do not think there was. I don't know what the problem was the first day because as I was better able to get about I observed the nursing activity on all shifts. They were busy, conscientious, dedicated, and very serious about taking care of medications, checking orders, passing on bits of information to each shift. I can only guess that there is some problem somewhere in the systems review that could make it possible for a post-operative patient not to get some kind of regular checking every hour or two, and some kind of special attention, or at least inquiry, as to well-being and comfort.

One final little note which perhaps should have some cross-reference to housekeeping. On the Sunday before I was discharged I happened to make use of a urinal during the night. Having partially filled the vessel, I placed it on the floor next to my bedside cabinet. Monday morning I was amused to find the housekeeping service sweep around this partially filled urinal. Members of the nursing staff came and went without paying any attention to this partially filled urinal. On Tuesday morning I observed the same thing with the housekeeping staff, and through Tuesday another three shifts of the nursing service passed over the urinal's presence. On Tuesday evening, a female visitor carefully averted her eyes from this partially filled urinal until I pointed it out to set her somewhat at ease, explaining that I was then in the midst of an experiment. I was discharged from the hospital Thursday morning and at about ten o'clock I confessed to the nurses on duty that I had not said anything to anybody about this partially filled urinal which had stood there since Sunday night but that I felt compelled to do so at this juncture since it might conceivably upset any patient who followed me into that room if that urinal was still there. The nurses were visibly upset by this. It was certainly not my intent to upset them and it was not a perverted sense of whimsy that led me to leave the urinal there. It does indicate, however, that there is some confusion about responsibility between the nursing service and the housekeeping service or else the nursing staff is either unobservant or embarrassed. I can't believe either of the latter and must confess being baffled as to how this could occur.

It is, indeed, difficult to understand the variation of level of service among this group of bright, alert, pleasant and conscientious professionals. Indeed, I would not hesitate to employ any of them to pursue duties in my office or in any institution for which I might have some responsibility. How and why these things can occur is a matter that deserves considerable study. Indeed, it is a matter that requires more study than chastising. My guess is that a look at the work of the nurses would indicate some fault or deficiency with the systems that have been designed for them to follow.

On Food Service

The food service at this hospital had an error incidence of between 20 and 30 percent. This is almost beyond belief. Certainly no less than one in five meals, and more likely one in three meals, were served with either small or great errors. These errors included no meal being served at all despite the fact that no stop had been ordered; dry toast being served my roommate, who was on a very strict liquid diet; failure to include part of my roommate's meal, although his caloric intake was a matter of grave concern to the physicians; minor absurdities such as soup being served both of us with no spoons on either tray and none available on the floor; the use of a palatized system for keeping hot things hot with a palate omitted from under the plate; or the sending up of a plate with a hot palate under it and nothing on the plate; and on to inappropriate silverware, no silverware, the almost unbelievable use of picnic type plastic ware for eating, etc.

One obvious difficulty, in my opinion, lay in the nature of the form used for selecting menu choices. While this form was adequate for telling the cooks what they had to prepare on the following day (it was a mark sensed form which could be run through an IBM machine to calculate how many portions of each item were necessary), its layout was such that anyone trying to check the trays on a trayveyor system against the form would either go blind or out of his mind after looking at about ten of these.

Another problem, I believe, lay in the inadequate communication between the floor dietitians and the kitchen dietitians. While my own situation was not terribly important so far as diet was concerned, that of my roommate was. He was on a very strict liquid diet. He was losing weight steadily. This was a matter of considerable concern to his physicians. It was not until his physician complained bitterly about the inattention to his patient's food that the dietary service made some sincere attempt to develop foods my roommate might conceivably enjoy. Some of the choices that they gave him can only be described as almost vile. While taste is a personal matter, it is hard to believe that anyone who has ever tasted baby food liver would try to offer this as being a tasty dish. Despite the fact that my roommate had indicated he could not abide a bacon flavor in blended eggs, he was served blended eggs with bacon. I had to protest this kind of neglect and oversight to two dietitians and a physician before I felt any impression had been made in the dietary service.

I cannot believe that an error rate anywhere close to that which the dietary service endured would be tolerated for as long as 24 hours in the hospital's pharmacy or in their central supply, or if operating rooms were inappropriately prepared for scheduled operations with improper tools, utensils, etc. available for the surgeon. I would feel that the situation in the dietary service in this hospital is so bad as to represent a virtual crisis because it is so close to almost total breakdown. I have no doubt that there are patients being hurt, and seriously hurt, because of this high error rate. I observed this with my own roommate who, because of errors in one day, suffered a higher weight loss than any other day during the seventeen days that I was there. How much of his weight loss was due to error, lack of imagination, lack of concern on the part of the dietary service, is hard to assess, but I am convinced that some of his weight loss must be ascribed to the inadequacies of the dietary service.

On Housekeeping

Perhaps the best and worst that might be said about the housekeeping service, at least so far as my room was concerned, is that it was lackadaisical and unenthusiastic. I only saw people dry-mopping the room during the seventeen days I was there. At no time was the floor of the bathroom wet mopped, much less the floor of the room I was in. I did observe walls and the corridors and some other rooms being scrubbed down. This appeared to be on some kind of schedule. However, so far as room cleaning was concerned, it was not much.

I would comment on one other minor point. My room was located just outside the service closet. Housekeeping personnel apparently gathered there at 7:30 in the morning to gather up their supplies preparatory to emptying wastepaper baskets or doing whatever they had to do. They made no effort whatsoever to modulate their voices. The gathering was apparently a noisy, social occasion. They, not infrequently, called to each other halfway down the hall and at that hour this was somewhat disturbing.

On Social Services

My experience leads me to believe that, at least in this hospital, a new approach · to hospital social services may be called for. It is insufficient to rely upon the patient to call out for help from social services. The plain fact of the matter is that most patients are not aware of what a social worker can or can't do for them. On the other hand, a social services department has much to offer many patients who need help from a professional social worker. This is going to become increasingly more the case as older people avail themselves of the benefits of Medicare. Take my roommate, for example. This man was hospitalized for treatment of what he knew might be a fatal illness. He was a man who was very much alone despite contacts with some relatives. He was a man who had suffered the loss of his spouse recently. He was a man who, like one-third of all people sixty-five and over, spoke with a foreign accent and who might have increasing difficulty with English as tension, stress, and anxiety levels increased.

My roommate was a man who said to me one day, "I suppose my whole life will have to change now. I will have to get a nurse or a housekeeper in to live with me. I will have to get somebody to prepare my food. Maybe I won't be able to drive any more." He discussed the provisions of his will with me indicating some anxieties about what his relatives might think about this or that provision. He was not a poor man by any means. Indeed, he was quite well-off. He had some plans to go to Florida in the fall and then to Israel in the spring to visit a nephew. He was concerned about approaching his physician about what he could or couldn't do. This man was a bundle of anxieties. Many of these things could have been anticipated from his admission form and by some kind of routine communication from the nurses to the social services department.

However, I doubt that there was any provision for communication except in terms of the most overt kind of cry for help from the patient. My roommate was a man who could have benefited from some effort to find him a chess partner. He had brought a chess board and chess pieces and a chess book with him. This was something that meant a great deal to him. He, unfortunately, in me drew a partner who not only did not know how to play chess but, for whatever reasons, did not want to learn. No volunteer came to play chess, no group workers appeared to help this lone person. I wonder how many others on how many other floors were as ambulatory as he and who were as alone and as anxious, who put up not only with days and days and days of worry and anxiety, but perhaps with weeks. When I left the hospital he was completing his third week, and would probably be in the hospital a fourth. His days had very little to fill them after his fifteen or twenty minutes of treatment and fewer minutes than that of attention from his physician.

I have one other comment that probably is not relevant to social services but does have something to do with accommodating to non-medical, non-nursing patient needs. As noted, my roommate was alone and had very few visitors. Rather than wear the unironed hospital pajamas, he changed during the day into pajamas of his own. However, he had no one to make arrangements for the laundering of these pajamas. He was an extraordinarily meticulous and neat individual and this concerned him. It was only when my wife suggested that she would take the pajamas to the laundry and I would arrange for a friend to pick them up that any provision was made for this at all. It is not sufficient to rely on informal methods for this kind of service. It is also insufficient to expect the inarticulate to call for this kind of service or request it on their own. Hospital staffs must be somewhat more sensitive than they appear to be to these kinds of non-medical, non-nursing service needs.

I believe that social services departments in hospitals must look beyond their traditional concerns and begin to look at these elderly, lonely patients who may be facing a health situation that will introduce major changes in their lives, their relationships, and their lifestyles. Much of this can be picked up in very simple ways. However, the relationship that a social worker enters into will not come easy as those who work in the field of aging can attest. But the older person is captive and he has time, and social service has a great deal to offer in helping him and perhaps his family adjust to required altered modes of living, the prospect of death, of diminished energy, and diminished ability.

As a first step, I would urge hospitals to take a hard look at the characteristics of the older people who are coming in through their doors, regarding well their length of stay, their marital status, the number of visitors they have, ascertaining on whom they rely, and trying to ferret out what it is that concerns them about their hospitalization.

No one should mistake the purpose of this memorandum. It is not to criticize or complain. I went to this hospital because I sought out a particular surgeon. I secured excellent medical care and, for the most part, excellent nursing care. My goal was to correct a bodily defect through surgical intervention.

This goal will have been achieved. Despite what deficiencies may have existed that I have described above, measured in terms of the goal established one must report success. However, not all cases are that simple and in not all cases are the results so direct. In some cases those good results are achieved only at the cost of a certain amount of anguish and aggravation. Perhaps this memorandum can serve to avoid some of that anguish.

Other cases, however, will not "succeed," and failure may be ascribed to failures in the system. This memorandum is in part addressed to that possibility. Beyond that, I think that all of us have some duty to try to improve on what may already be a reasonably good operation. Here again, this is among my prime purposes in writing all of this down. My main hope is that this memorandum will serve some constructive purpose.

Whose Hospital?

Anthony R. Kovner

Tony DeFalco, a 42-year-old electrical engineer, and president of the board of trustees of Brendan Hospital in Lockhart, East State, wondered what he had done wrong. Why had this happened to him again? What should he do now? The trustees had voted, at first 10 to 6 and then unanimously, to fire Don Wherry, the new chief executive officer. Brendan Hospital had hired Wherry, who had been DeFalco's personal choice from over 200 candidates just 18 months before. DeFalco had told the trustees that he shared the burdens of managing Brendan Hospital with Wherry, that there was no way of dissociating Wherry's decisions from his own decisions. So in a way, DeFalco pondered, the board should have fired him, too.

Tony DeFalco had lived in Lockhart all his life, and he loved the town, commuting one-and-one-half hours each day to his office at National Electric. Lockhart was one of the poorest towns in the poorest county in central East State, with a population of about 50,000, of which 30 percent were Italian, 25 percent Puerto-Rican, and 10 percent Jewish. The leading industries in town were lumber, auto parts manufacturing, and agriculture.

On June 7, 1979, Joe Black, president of the Brendan Hospital medical staff, had called Tony DeFalco, telling him that some doctors and nurses had met over the weekend and that they were going to hold a mass meeting at the hospital to discuss charges against CEO Wherry. DeFalco had called Wherry immediately in Montreal, Canada, where Wherry was giving a lecture to healthcare administration faculty about the relationship between the chief executive officer and the board of trustees. Wherry was as shocked as DeFalco had been and returned immediately to Lockhart. That night DeFalco and

Wherry went to a hospital foundation meeting near where the mass meeting was being held in the hospital cafeteria.

DeFalco and Wherry had been planning the foundation meeting for several months now. It had been scheduled and rescheduled so that all eight of the prominent townspeople could attend. The key reasons behind forming the foundation were: to enlist the energies of community leaders in hospital fund-raising; to thereby free the hospital board for more effective policymaking; and to shield hospital donations from the state rate-setting authority. Brendan Hospital had held a successful first annual horse show the previous fall, netting $10,000 and creating goodwill for the hospital, largely through the efforts of DeFalco and two dedicated physicians who owned the stable and dedicated the show and all proceeds to the hospital. Because this was a very important meeting, and because they had not been invited to attend the mass meeting, DeFalco and Wherry decided to attend the foundation meeting. There, they elicited a great deal of verbal support for the foundation, and for DeFalco's leadership. The community leaders were familiar with the problems of employee discontent in their own businesses and with the political maneuverings of former Brendan medical staffs. It would all calm down, no doubt. The wife of the town's leading industrialist said she appreciated DeFalco's frankness in sharing the hospital's problems with them.

But, of course, everything was not yet calm. The mass meeting was held and a petition signed to get rid of Wherry. The petition was signed by half the medical staff and by half the employees as well. A leadership committee of four doctors and nurses demanded Wherry's immediate resignation, and it was rumored that if the board didn't vote Wherry out, the committee wanted the board's resignation as well. Brendan Hospital was being site-visited for JCAH accreditation that Thursday and Friday. A board meeting was held on Wednesday afternoon, before the site visit. After much discussion, a decision emerged to meet with the staff and employee representatives on the following Monday. The accreditation site visit somehow went smoothly.

The four doctor and nurse representatives met with the board on Monday afternoon, stating that they could not speak for the others. They delivered the petition to DeFalco, who read it to the trustees. The petition stated that the undersigned demanded Wherry's resignation because he was "incompetent, devious, lacked leadership, had shown unprofessional conduct, and had committed negligent acts." The representatives would not discuss the matter at that time. They had been delegated only to deliver the petition. Thus, DeFalco scheduled another board meeting for the following Wednesday afternoon to hear all the charges by all the accusers, and to allow Wherry to confront his accusers, thirteen days after the mass meeting of June 8.

The meeting of June 22 was attended by eight physicians, eighteen registered nurses, five department heads, a laboratory supervisor, one dietary aide, and the medical staff secretary. (For an organization chart of Brendan Hospital see Appendix A.) Seventeen of the eighteen hospital trustees were in attendance, including Wherry, who was a member of the board. The meeting was held in the tasteful new boardroom of Brendan Hospital, complete with oak tables and plush burgundy carpeting. The committee's presentation is summarized as follows:

The Accusers' Charges

Perrocchio: The most important thing we have to discuss today is patient care. That's why all of us are here. Many of us are not here because we have a personal gripe, but because we want to do what's best for the patient.

Tully (department head): Mr. Wherry humiliated and intimidated three department heads, Mr. O'Brien, Mrs. Williamson, and Mr. Queen.

Pappas (department head): There is a bad morale problem in the laundry.

Patrocelli (supervisor): Laboratory morale is low. There are too many people in other departments and not enough personnel in our department. Companies who deliver to us have put us on COD.

Fong (department head): Mr. Wherry humiliated Mr. Queen.

Frew: There has been a problem in staffing new areas of the hospital. We were told that these would be adequately staffed. I realize they haven't opened yet.

Tontellino: Several months ago a nursing survey was sent around by Mr. Wherry, and we all sent in our responses. We have received no response from Mr. Wherry about the survey.

Carter (RN): We need more help on the floors.

Greenberg: Insensitivity is the problem. The administrator, as you can see from all the comments made so far, is insensitive to the people who work in the hospital.

Santengelo (medical staff secretary): The director of volunteers' salary should have been explained to the rest of us. Employees should continue to get the $5 and $10 Christmas bonus. It means a lot to many of them. Mr. Wherry has created a whole lot of unnecessary paperwork. I don't feel he heard what we were telling him.

Lafrance (RN): There has been a lack of communication between administration and employees. Mr. Wherry actually has asked people to give him the solution to a problem they presented to him.

Shaw (RN and former director of nursing): Mr. Wherry used four letter words in his office with me. He called one of our attending physicians a . . .

Levari (RN): When there was a bomb scare, Mr. Wherry came to the hospital and stayed for twenty minutes. Then he left before the police came, which I definitely think was wrong.

Leon (RN): It took Mr. Wherry ten months to call a meeting with the head nurses. Problems in nursing have to be solved around here by the nursing department.

Kelly (RN and assistant director): The problem has been lack of communication. I was humiliated when I presented a memo to Mr. Wherry about increases in operating room expenses. He said he couldn't understand what was in the memo, although it was right in front of him. His whole manner was rude.

Phillips (RN and assistant director): When the state inspector came on one of her inspections, she said that Mr. Wherry should be dumped.

Santengelo (medical staff secretary): He told Dr. Burns one thing and me another when we needed extra help in my office.

Bernstein (RN): Mr. Wherry was evasive and showed a lack of concern. He asked me for my suggestions. I told him to put an ad in the paper to get more help, and it was in the next day. Nurses were not present at administrative meetings.

Brown (department head): Mr. Wherry said Dr. Black would also have to sign an x-ray equipment request for $100,000. That is poor leadership.

Ferrari (RN): I didn't like the tone of his response when I called him at home to ask about treating a Jehovah's Witness in the emergency room. When we call Mr. Queen, the associate administrator, we nurses never experience that kind of problem.

Lashof (department head): I felt intimidated by Mr. Wherry. The hospital has a morale problem which interferes with patient care.

Brown (department head): He said to me "If you can't handle the problem" (we were having in X-ray) I'll find someone who can."

Charlorre (RN): I've had a problem with my insurance and the personnel department still hasn't gotten back to me for three weeks now. I am divorced and I have a little girl, and it's really creating a hardship for me. I don't understand why Mr. Gonzales, the personnel director, hasn't gotten back to me. I've called him about it many times.

Lafrance (RN): Mr. Wherry sounded upset and annoyed when I called him at home about the electrical fire in maternity.

Gerew: The problem is communication. Mr. Wherry promised something and he didn't deliver. I have been working here for three years trying to develop a first-class radiology department. How can we cut costs and improve service in the outpatient department? I asked for help from fiscal affairs and I didn't get any.

Lavich: The family no longer has any confidence in its father. There was a unanimous vote of no confidence for Mr. Wherry in my department.

Greenberg: Mr. Wherry has a repressive style. There has been a tremendous turnover of personnel in the nursing department since he became the administrator.

Mendez: There is poor morale at the hospital. The nurses are upset. Mr. Wherry used derogatory language concerning foreign medical graduates. This was in the student administrative resident's report on what to do about the emergency room. Let's remove what is causing the problem.

Black (president of the medical staff): Department heads should be on board committees. No one came around and told department heads that they were appreciated. People at Shop-N-Bag make more money than nurses. Our medical people want to be appreciated, too.

Frew: Tony DeFalco, the board president, is seen as being in Mr. Wherry's pocket. There must be accountability for the situation which arose. I have no personal grievance. Accountability starts at the top.

Black: Dr. Fanchini was behind a good deal of what I was doing. A lot of critical things have happened making for a crisis situation. Dr. Simba was hired to head up the emergency room, without adequate participation of the medical staff. Dr. Fanchini resigned as a board member. Dr. Burns resigned as president of the medical staff because of his personal problems. Mr. Wherry said that Dr. Severio was not really a cardiologist. The radiologists at Clarksville Hospital asked for emergency privileges. What made the medical staff unhappy was when Mr. Wherry said we weren't going to get a CT scanner and when he said that there were no problems in nursing morale. At the meeting of the medical executive committee held this Monday night, June 20, the committee reaffirmed our lack of support for Mr. Wherry, giving him a vote of no confidence by a vote of ten for the motion, one against, and one abstaining.

Listening to the doctors and nurses, DeFalco felt as if he was a spectator watching a Greek tragedy. The committee representatives left the boardroom. DeFalco remembered when the board had met in the old private dining room only two years before, voting to dismiss the previous administrator of 22 years, Phil Drew, because Drew allegedly hadn't kept up with the times, some doctors said he had sexually harassed several of the nurses, and the hospital wasn't doing well financially. Drew had been a good man, and Tony DeFalco had promised himself that he would do everything in his power to prevent this from happening again.

Wherry's Defense

"First I'd like to go through the state of the hospital, as it was when I got here," Wherry began nervously. And yet DeFalco thought Wherry seemed perfectly assured of himself, confident in the rightness of his cause. That was probably one of the things the doctors held against him—besides, Don had attended Princeton undergraduate and Harvard Business School, and had worked for a government regulatory agency in hospital cost containment before taking the Brendan job.

Wherry: There was bad leadership in the nursing department and in several other departments, a lack of medical staff leadership, and few competent department heads. Nursing is a difficult occupation. Morale is always a problem in this department. These are young people with children, working evenings, nights, and weekends, and the work is physically, emotionally, and administratively demanding. The doctors at this hospital are like doctors in other hospitals like Brendan, fearful of anything that threatens to affect their livelihood or freedom. I can understand that. But there is a small, embittered group with axes to grind against me. [For a list of 1978 Brendan Hospital goals and accomplishments, see Appendix B. For 1979 Brendan Hospital goals, see Appendix C.]

I have been busy with the finances of the hospital and in improving external relationships with the Hispanics, state officials, and other groups. Mel Queen, the associate administrator, has been busy with the new construction and moving into our new $5 million wing. We've had a new director of nursing on board for five weeks now, and I wish that everyone would have just given her a chance. Dr. Burns' resignation as president of the medical staff didn't help me any, and I have had a director of personnel, Gonzales, with acute personal problems, which has been a problem for me too. . . . Next, it's quite unusual for someone to have to defend himself on the spot to a list of specific charges which I have been waiting for these past thirteen days and just have been made aware of now. I think the way this whole thing has been handled by the doctor and nurse ringleaders is disgraceful. The charges they have made are largely not true and could not be proven even if they were true. Even if the charges are true to a substantial extent, there is still not sufficient reason for your discharging me, certainly not suddenly as they are demanding you to.

The doctors are out to get me because I'm doing the job you've been paying me to do, what I'm evaluated on, and for which I received a very good evaluation and a big raise at the end of last year, presumably because I was doing a good job. (For Wherry's evaluation, see Appendix D; for DeFalco's raise letter, see Appendix E.) Certainly none of you have told me to stop doing what I have been doing to assure quality, contain costs and improve service. During the past year I gathered information for the medical staff on a new reappointment worksheet so that reappointments aren't made on a rubber stamp process every two years. I pointed out the problems that the low inpatient census in pediatrics would create in retaining the beds in the years to come. I obtained model rules and regulations for the medical staff and shared these with the president, Dr. Black. I questioned the effectiveness of the tissue committee, which hasn't been meeting, and when it has met, whose minutes are perfunctory. I questioned the performance of the audit committee after our delegated status under PSRO was placed in question by a visiting physician, Dr. Lordi. I suggested we explore mandated physician donations to the hospital, as was passed and implemented two years ago by another East State hospital. When patients made complaints about doctors I took these up with the respective chiefs of departments. I investigated the assertion by a lab technician that tests were being reported and not done by the laboratory. I questioned and had to renegotiate remuneration of pathologists and radiologists, all with knowledge of the president of the board, Mr. DeFalco, and I have done nothing without involving the medical executive committee.

I have been involved in the lengthy and frustrating process of getting support from other hospitals for a CT scanner and in justifying financial feasibility of the CT scanner at this hospital. I have suggested ways to re-cruit needed physicians into Lockhart and have shared with the staff other approaches used by East State hospitals, such as a guaranteed income for the first year. I followed up a trustee's question about the appropriateness of fetal monitoring with the chief of obstetrics and gynecology, and worked out a satisfactory response to poor ophthalmology coverage in the emergency room with the chief of ophthalmology. I became involved in trying to convince one of our three pathologists not to resign because of a run-in with the chief of pathology. I have to get after physicians who do not indicate final diagnosis or complete their charts on time, since this delays needed cash flow for the hospital. I suggested that the hospital develop a model program for providing day hospital and other care to the elderly and chronically ill, and sought the cooperation of State University in designing a research protocol to measure the need for such services. This was resented by several members of the staff, although we have not gone ahead with the State research program pending staff approval, or, if they disapprove, I said we would not go ahead with it.

I initiated a study of how we can prevent malpractice at the hospital, conveyed board disapproval of radiology equipment, which we had scheduled to buy but couldn't afford because other radiology equipment broke down in an unforeseen way. There are several very difficult physicians on the medical executive committee who have never gotten along with any administrator or with other physicians. I am the one who has to discuss with the surgeons and the radiologists ways to decrease costs in their units when these costs are way above the state medians and we have to reduce them or face financial penalties.

As far as nursing goes, here is a list of what I have done: I have met with all shifts, with head nurses, with supervisors, and regularly with the director and assistant directors. I hired a new director and fired an old assistant director whom the nurses said showed favoritism, lied to them, and overpromised. This was opposed, by the way, by Dr. Fanchini, former director of obstetrics and gynecology. I hired an expert nursing consultant to help us develop appropriate goals and ways of meeting these goals. I was in the process of obtaining the services of an operations research consultant, at no cost to the hospital, to help us with our scheduling problems. We implemented a study done by an administrative resident on improved staffing and scheduling. I pointed out all the problems of authoritarian leadership, lack of adequate quality assurance programs, and lack of appropriate scheduling and budgeting to the previous nursing director, which is why she had to be demoted. Mrs. Shaw always tried to do her best, but she lacked the proper education and skills. I obtained fifteen additional approved nursing positions, including one additional full-time RN in inservice and an additional $80,000 for inservice, from the state rate-setters, something which no one has been able to do at this hospital for the past eight years. Our expenditures in nursing are already above the state median. I obtained a staffing plan from another hospital for the director of nursing and influenced her to distribute a questionnaire to all nurses to better find out their feelings and ideas.

I could go through each of the charges made by the people assembled here, but it won't really prove anything. Yes, I did call a doctor a . . . in my office. Yes, I did leave the hospital after the bomb scare before the police came, but only after I was convinced that it was a scare. I had a meeting to go to in Urban City, and I called one hour later to see that everything was all right. I think it is significant that none of the department heads supposedly humiliated by me showed up at this meeting. You have asked me to resign, but I'm not going to resign. That would not solve the hospital's problems. Firing me will not solve the bad nursing morale here or the doctor distrust. It will show the doctors and nurses and the community who runs this hospital. Is it the board of trustees or some doctors and nurses (the nurses are mainly being used by the doctors)? Whose head will these doctors be asking for the next time they want to get rid of somebody? The bond issue set for next month that could refinance our debt on the new wing will not go through if you fire me. And we shall have a $355,000 payment to make in August which will be difficult to meet.

"Does anybody have any questions?" DeFalco asked the other trustees. There were a few questions, but nothing significant, no major contradictions of anything Wherry had said. A vote was taken to clear Wherry of the charges without rebuttal, and this passed 7 in favor, 5 against, with 4 abstentions. Then the trustees asked Wherry to leave the room, and told him that they would make a decision.

That evening, after dinner with his wife and teenagers, DeFalco watched a baseball game on television. He couldn't get his mind off that Wednesday night board meeting, the vote 10 to 6 against Wherry, and the ultimate unanimous vote to dismiss him with two months' severance. During the previous week, DeFalco had made it his business to discuss the Don Wherry situation with the other sixteen trustees (Wherry and he made eighteen). As best as he could recollect, the following was the essence of their comments to him.

Board Comments

Clock (age 55, life insurance salesman, first vice president of the board, former mayor, and DeFalco's long-time confidant): I have been one of Don Wherry's strongest supporters, since he got here and before he got here. I was a member of the search committee which selected Don, as you remember. I still like Don personally, really I do, but it has become obvious to me, at least, that Don can no longer manage the hospital. Whether Don is right or wrong, the docs don't like him. (Wherry told DeFalco that Clock sold a lot of life insurance to a lot of doctors.) Don's biggest mistakes have been in not firing Mel Queen, the associate administrator, who never has supported him properly, and Winnie Shaw, the ex-director of nursing whom he should never have kept around and I told him so.

Gotthuld (age 50, second vice president of the hospital board, president of the board of Preston College, and wife of a beer distributor): I have been spending one or two weeks out of every month in Vermont, you know, George, where we bought a distributorship, and last year Sam and I spent six months on a luxury liner trip around the world. So I really don't know what's going on that well. As chairman of the executive committee, we gave Don a good evaluation and if he isn't acting properly as chief executive officer, then at least part of the fault is ours. I see no reason to fire Don abruptly because of these alleged charges.

Lance (age 45, president of a local lumber company, treasurer of the hospital, and chairman of the buildings and grounds committee): I have always been one of Don Wherry's closest friends, although he may not admit it now. I think Don could do an excellent job managing a university hospital, but that he definitely cannot do the job here at Brendan and that we should get rid of him now. Don might care more than anyone else, certainly more than I do, about the welfare of the hospital employees, but Don just hadn't communicated that to them.

Gonce (65 years old, RN, secretary of the hospital, recently returned for the board meeting from University Hospital in Urban City where she was recovering from a heart attack): Tony, you know I fought bitterly against Don Wherry's coming to Brendan in the first place, voted then for Mel Queen, the associate administrator to do the job, and I vote for him now to do a better job than Don Wherry. Don should be working for the government somewhere, not in a small town. Mel Queen will make an excellent administrator of Brendan Hospital. We should have given it to him in the first place.

Giancarlo (age 60, president of a local canning firm, newly elected to the board in January): I don't know much about the facts of the situation, Tony; I like Don Wherry personally, but obviously the doctors and many of the employees are unhappy with him. They must be listened to. It doesn't seem that anything they are complaining about is new or isolated.

Gonzales (age 40, secondary school teacher, was one of Don Wherry's strongest supporters): I see what Don has done to meet with all the Hispanic leaders without any crisis, to hear out our problems and respond to us. Don has reorganized and improved services in the emergency room, hired a Spanish-speaking social work assistant, increased the number of minority supervisors. I am not that impressed, really, by these charges. There's no meat to them. I think this is just a bunch of doctors trying to get rid of Don as they got rid of Mr. Drew, the last CEO, and I do not think the board should bow down to them this time.

Peppino (age 34, senior bank vice president): Knowing Don Wherry as I do, I can understand a lot of the charges and sympathize with those making the complaints. Don Wherry is cold and authoritative, and if he knows so much, maybe that isn't what the job needs anyway. Mel Queen can run the hospital perfectly well, I'm convinced of that. And if the doctors are going to stop admitting patients as they threaten to do, they must feel very strongly about Don Wherry. It's important to calm the doctors down and get on with business as usual, and the sooner the better. Don Wherry will have no problem finding a job somewhere else. Maybe he was going to leave Lockhart anyway after a few more years.

Black (age 45, president of the medical staff): We have to get rid of this guy. He's nothing but trouble. I tried to work with him, but the guys don't like him. Maybe it's because he went to Princeton or something. He gives the guys this feeling that he feels superior to us. He's the big time administrator and we're the lowly or something doctors. We'd much prefer Mel Queen running the hospital. We don't have to put up with this Wherry guy, and now's the time to get rid of him.

Romano (age 50, president of a lumber company, newly elected to the board in January): I feel the way Lew Giancarlo does. I never thought being elected to this board would involve all these problems, and I'm certainly spending more time on this darn hospital than I would like to be spending. It's a tough thing for this Wherry guy. I like Don personally, but I really think we're going to have more problems with him than without him.

Levine (age 45, attorney, newly elected to the board in January): I think this is disgraceful what we're doing to Don. I don't like the way the whole thing was done, even if Don has made mistakes. You don't treat an employee this way, certainly not the chief executive officer. But I don't think that Don has handled it right, either. He should have gone to the mass meeting and defended himself. He should have organized people to speak on his behalf. That's the advice I would have given Don as a lawyer. And I think it's a darn shame this has to happen. It doesn't have to happen really, if someone would only stand up and fight for Don and Don's cause. I'm doing the best that I can, but I've only been on the board a short time, and I feel I'm therefore limited in what I can do.

Morrissey (age 47, housewife): Don and his wife Sue are personal friends of mine, but I can't let that get in the way of making the right decision for the hospital. Don is certainly a brilliant guy who cares about people and doesn't want to see the patient or the consumer taken advantage of. He wants to do all the right things and he has done a lot of the right things. The hospital is a safer, warmer, financially more sound place than it was when Don took over. I'm certainly going to vote for Don. I'm sorry, but I don't feel I know enough to be really energetic about this.

Viggiani (age 60, owner of a large real estate firm and chairman of the county Democratic Party): I think it's a terrible thing what they're doing to Don. It's just like with the other guy, Phil Drew. This guy has always been there when we needed him. He works night and day. If anything's the matter, then it must be our fault because this guy has been doing what we've been telling him to do. He hasn't done anything without telling the doctors and us first. I think it's a disgrace.

Asselta (age 70, general practitioner): The staff just doesn't like him. I like Don Wherry. I know he's been trying to do the right thing. I've tried to help Don, after I made sure of him, every way I can. You know my wife has been very sick and I haven't been able to attend to hospital affairs lately as I would like. I guess I'll go along with the majority, either way.

Goldman (age 61, chief of ob-gyn, newly elected to the board in January): I don't think the man knows how to manage the hospital, asking the employees to come up with the solutions to their own problems. That's bad management. Our group is against him.

Catrambone (age 50, director of a large funeral home): Tony, I'm only sorry I won't be at the meeting to speak for Don. There's a right and a wrong, and I can tell the difference. Ask yourself who is right and who is wrong and you've got to vote for Don Wherry. I happen to think he's a pretty fair manager to boot. I wish you would count my vote. Since my open heart surgery, I've got to be in Rochester, Minnesota for my annual heart examination.

Stuart (age 41, senior vice president of the same bank of which Mrs. Peppino is assistant vice president.) [Don Wherry had told DeFalco that Stuart and Peppino were against him because he gave all the bank business per finance committee recommendation to a competing bank.]: I don't like Don Wherry. I never have. I served with him on the personnel committee and we were usually in disagreement. Don always made me feel somehow that I was ignorant, that he felt himself superior to me. This is not how he should have acted. And I'm sure a lot of the employees feel the same way about Don that I do.

Appendix A Brendan Hospital Organizations Chart, Board of Trustees

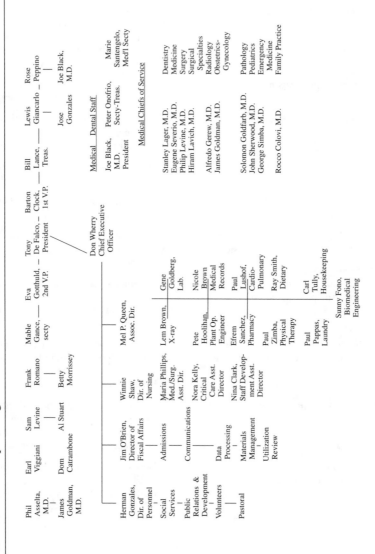

Appendix B   Brendan Hospital 1978 Goals and Accomplishments from
1978 Annual Report

1978 Goals	*1978 Accomplishments*
1. Stabilize hospital finances	• $75,000 surplus • Improved Medicaid and Blue Cross reimbursement • Expenditures reduced in line with lower than expected occupancy
2. Increase fund-raising	• Modernization fund pledges on target • Successful first annual horse show
3. Improve hospital morale	• Regular employee-administration meetings • Regular publication of *Brendan News*
4. Improve quality of nursing care	• High patient evaluations in survey • New director of nursing recruited
5. Organize department of emergency medicine	• Department organized and Dr. George Simba recruited as chief
6. Establish effective management information and control system	• Implemented auditors' recommendation • Evaluating new data processing alternatives
7. Increase communication with Spanish-speaking community	• Several meetings held with Hispanic leaders • Increased Hispanic staff in patient areas, including social services
8. Increase accountability of medical departments for quality assurance	• Board resolution requiring annual reports • Joint conference committee and trustee seminar for better communication between medical staff and trustees
9. Increase community participation in long-range planning	• Four community members added to long-range planning committee • Wide distribution of annual report with attendance encouraged at annual meeting
10. On schedule, on budget, fully accredited new wing	• New wing scheduled to open in April 1979 • Building is roughly within budget and on schedule

Appendix C   1979 Brendan Hospital Goals (from 1978 Annual Report)

1. Stabilize hospital finances and improve cash flow
2. Improve board–administration–medical staff communication
3. Increase hospital involvement of Spanish-speaking community
4. Fill administrative vacancies and recruit needed medical staff
5. Increase pediatric and obstetrical inpatient occupancy
6. Accomplish complete availability of new wing by April and obtain full hospital accreditation
7. Establish quality assurance programs for all professional departments
8. Establish productivity and efficiency goals for all hospital departments
9. Develop an operational long-range plan including time and dollar estimates for new programs
10. Continue to contain increases in hospital costs

Appendix D   Summary of CEO Evaluation (November 25, 1978)

	Rating 1–5 (1 is high, 5 is low)	
I. Goal Achievement	Self	Avg. Trustee
1. Stabilize hospital finance	1	2.7
2. Increase fund-raising	3	3.6
3. Improve hospital morale	3	4.9
4. Improve quality of nursing care	1	3.7
5. Organize emergency room department	1	2.9
6. Establish an effective management information and control system	2	2.1
7. Maintain on-schedule, on-budget west wing building program	3	2.3
8. Establish plan for utilization of west wing and integration with total hospital operations	3	2.1
9. Increase communications with the growing Spanish-speaking community	1	3.1
10. Increase accountability of medical departments for quality assurance	1	3.1
11. Prepare to obtain three-year hospital accreditation upon completion of west wing	3	1.9
12. Increase community participation in hospital long-range planning	1	2.2

CEO Remarks:
1. CEO is goal-oriented.

Continued

2. He needs to spend yet more time developing consensus and persuading key stakeholders and earning their respect.

Trustee Remarks:
1. Many of these "specifics" are difficult for an outside director to judge.
2. I think CEO's contributions are acceptable except in items 3 and 4, where they should have been significantly greater.
3. Morale is a question.
4. CEO is doing a fine job for Brendan.
5. CEO's capability is great for achieving all goals. Sometimes his motives are not understood, and some obstacles are not of his doing.
6. The answers to some of these questions are based more on perceptions than actual knowledge.

President's Remarks:
I agree that the CEO is goal-oriented. He has attained goals we have given him about as well as anyone could reasonably expect.

II. System Maintenance   2   3.5

CEO Remarks:
1. Given what the CEO was hired to do, a certain amount of distrust is inevitable.
2. The CEO tries diligently to establish regular and continuing dialogue with all key hospital groups and individuals.

Trustee Remarks:
1. Greatest weaknesses in this category are in maintaining adequate commitment of employees to organizational goals and developing adequate trust between management and medical staff.
2. The board is not made aware of exactly the number of employees needed and the department that has this need. There seems to be a feeling of unrest among the administrative staff (department heads). Trust between management and medical staff is currently very poor.
3. CEO's capabilities are limitless, but I feel he has developed a schism between himself and the medical staff.
4. Small areas of difference need to be cleared by better communication and understanding of mutual problems. Main problem area is with doctor contracts.
5. I suspect that the only positive factor in the above list would be "maintaining adequate administrative and control systems."

Continued

President's Remarks:

1. Our "hospital system" has undoubtedly provided sufficient patient care of adequate quality at reasonable cost. I therefore believe the trustee evaluation to be too low in this area.
2. A mistrust of the administration by the medical staff does exist. I am also apprehensive about the "team play" of the administrative staff. We must address these problems in 1979.

III. Relationships with Important External Publics   1   2.1

CEO Remarks:

The hospital has done well with licensing, regulatory, and reimbursement agencies, and with other provider agencies during 1978. The CEO speaks frequently to consumer organizations and volunteer groups as well and has been well received.

Trustee Remarks:

1. The CEO has done an especially good job with third party payors.
2. This is definitely the CEO's strongest area.
3. Excellent record.

President's Remarks:

I am pleased with the CEO's accomplishments in this area.

IV. Management Roles

1. Interpersonal   3   3.6
2. Informational   1   2.4
3. Decisional   1   2.8

CEO's Remarks:

The CEO is intelligent and quick. He works long hours and is subject to constant pressures. He cannot possibly talk at length continuously with 18 trustees, 40 key doctors, 20 department heads, and other key personnel outside the hospital. He must try harder to be cheerful, quiet, friendly, and low-key.

Trustee Remarks:

1. I think the CEO has done a good job in 1978, especially in view of what he walked into.
2. The CEO has weakness in providing motivation, also in recognizing disturbances of uneasiness within the hospital

Continued

personnel, and in dealing with incompetent or unproductive personnel.

3. The CEO seems to be seeking many changes. His method for achieving this isn't always productive. The CEO has great potential, but doesn't seem to implement it well.
4. I'm not too sure if CEO is handling personnel adequately. Morale has not improved within the hospital.
5. The CEO has done and is doing an outstanding job. I am proud to work with him and would give him even higher marks if possible.
6. The CEO is excellent on a one-to-one basis. He handles groups well. He is anxious to please and to get cooperation.

President's Remarks:
1. Changes in staff personnel in 1978 have hampered the efficiency and effectiveness of this group. When stability of this group occurs, provided the right group has been chosen, improvement in hospital management will be most evident.
2. The dissemination of information is exceptional.
3. I have confidence in the decisions that are being made. I am not sure about their method of implementation.

V. President's Summary
1. Areas of evaluation:
   The CEO has exceeded my expectations. In sum total, I am extremely pleased with his accomplishments.
2. Strengths:
   Planning, establishing priorities, dealing with regulatory agencies, understanding and articulating hospital organization, financial management, intelligence, creativity, ability to negotiate, potential, sincerity, and directness.
3. Weaknesses:
   Impatience and aloofness (coldness).
4. Uncertainties:
   Evaluation of personnel, evaluation of situations, employee motivation, and nonpeer and subordinate relationships.
5. Recommendations:
   Attempt to gain trust and respect of medical staff.
   Improve trust and respect of employees.
   Refrain from reprimanding employees in presence of others.
   Work toward having assistant responsible for day-to-day operation of hospital.
   Continue to attempt to improve morale.
   Improve patience; realize that few people can match intelligence quotient.
   Continue to develop administrative staff.
6. Conclusion:
   The CEO has performed well in 1978. He has acceptably attained his goals.

Continued

As a new manager, he has been severely tested by the board of trustees, medical staff, and employees, and has withstood their challenge. I believe his inherent intelligence will allow him to correct any and all identifiable deficiencies.

The CEO's self-evaluation was extremely accurate. It is comforting to know that he has the ability to correctly assess his strengths and weaknesses.

The following elements will be necessary for his continued success:
1. Constructive advice and support by board of trustees.
2. Trust of medical staff.
3. Melding of administrative staff into stable, competent, and qualified team with common objectives.

Appendix E Letter from Tony Defalco to Don Wherry of January 10, 1979

Personal and Confidential

Mr. Don Wherry   January 10, 1979
Brendan Hospital
Lockhart, East State

Dear Don,

The Board of Trustees of Brendan Hospital, on January 8, 1979 unanimously approved a 10% increase in your annual salary along with a $500 increase in automobile allowance for 1979. The above increases will result in a per annum salary of $57,750 and an automobile allowance of $2,300. Your receipt of this letter provides you with the authority to make the stipulated adjustments effective January 1, 1979.

Our board believes that you have done an outstanding job as our Chief Executive Officer and hopes that the above increases have fairly rewarded your effort.

Very truly yours,

Tony DeFalco, President
Brendan Hospital, Board of Trustees

Short Case K

The Conflicted HMO Manager

Anthony R. Kovner

Bill Brown built up University Hospital's HMO over ten years so that now it had 100,000 members, and his boss Jim Edgar decided to sell the insurance part of the business (retaining the medical groups) because UH wasn't in the insurance business. Bill was asked to recruit some bidders, one of whom, Liberty National, Jim came to prefer because of their financial strength and excellent reputation. In the process of working with Liberty National, Bill learned that they wanted to hire him, after the sale, to be the president of their regional HMO activities. Bill told Jim what was likely to happen in this regard. The deal was subsequently approved by Bill's board (of the HMO) and by Jim's board (of the hospital). Two years after the sale; Bill works for Liberty and is making $5 million a year, while University is losing $5 million a year. Joe Kelly, University's new CEO, figures out that the contract that Bill Brown negotiated for University was highly favorable to Liberty and now University can't, for another nine years, get out of it.

Case Questions

- Did Brown act unethically? If so, how? What should Brown have done? Why didn't he do it?
- Did Edgar act competently? If not, what should he have done differently? Why didn't he do it?
- What should the University CEO, Joe Kelly, do now?

Short Case L

The Great Mosaic: Multiculturalism at Seaview Nursing Home

James Castiglione and Anthony R. Kovner

Alice O'Connor is the new director of the Seaview Nursing Home (SNH), a large investor-owned facility in Far West City, which provides services to 98 ethnic groups speaking 68 different languages. Most of the top management jobs at SNH are held by white females. Whereas there is a 23 percent Latino population in Far West City, Latinos hold only a 6 percent representation in the higher levels of management at SNH. SNH has an affirmative action program, and as a result, staff members at lower levels come from a wide range of backgrounds. 12 percent of SNH employees are classified as minorities.

According to her predecessor, Una Light, SNH has had an exemplary affirmative action program, promoting diversity awareness, hiring more minority staff at lower-level positions, and being responsive to the health needs of the minority populations served by the nursing home.

SNH has a diversity awareness training program that has been offered 14 times over the last two years. The need for this program has been assessed through internal surveys and interviews of all staff. The purpose of these meetings is to increase the level of awareness and sensitivity of the staff of SNH as service providers; to promote awareness within the organization and increase the level of informed cross-cultural interactions among staff; and to expose potential problems and keep them from increasing in severity.

Only 8 percent of students who graduated last year from local accredited schools of nursing or healthcare administration were minorities. Latinos accounted for only 3 percent of graduates.

As part of getting familiar with the organization, Ms. O'Connor has had conversations with each of SNH's middle managers. Anna Gonzales, who is Latino, feels that given the large minority population in the area, SNH is not doing enough to grant power to minority groups. She would like to be considered for the position of Deputy Director, currently occupied by a 60-year-old white female. Jim Leone, another of the middle managers, points out that white men have not occupied positions of power at SNH for the last 20 years, and that positions should be allocated strictly on the basis of merit.

Case Questions

- Do you feel that SNH has been doing an adequate job in managing diversity?
- What, if anything, do you think the new director should do differently?
- How useful is the concept of "minorities" in managing diversity?

Selected Bibliography

This bibliography on health services management cases is not intended to be exhaustive, but rather a beginning point for those in search of good cases. For sources on the topics of these cases, see our companion book of readings (Kovner and Neuhauser, *Health Services Management: A Book of Readings*, 6th Edition, Chicago: Health Administration Press, 1997).

I. Casebooks

Billington, George F. *Cases in Hospital Administration*. New York: School of Public Health and Administrative Medicine, Columbia University, 1959.

Brecher, Charles (ed.). *Managing Safety-Net Hospitals*. Chicago: Health Administration Press, 1993.

Coddington, Dean C., et al. *Making Integrated Health Care Work: Case Studies*. Englewood, CO: Center for Research in Ambulatory Care Administration, 1996.

Conrad, Douglas A., and Geoffrey A. Hoare. *Strategic Alignment: Managing Integrated Health Systems*. Chicago: Health Administration Press, 1993.

Griffith, John R. *The Moral Challenges of Health Care Management*. Chicago: Health Administration Press, 1993.

Herzlinger, Regina E. *Creating New Health Ventures: The Role of Management*. Gaithersburg, MD: Aspen, 1992.

Infeld, Donna Lind, and John R. Kress. *Cases in Long-Term Management*. Chicago: Health Administration Press, 1989, and vol. 2, 1995.

Kindig, David A., and Anthony R. Kovner, (eds.). *The Role of the Physician Executive: Cases and Commentary*. Chicago: Health Administration Press, 1992.

Rakich, Jonathon S., et al. *Cases in Health Services Management*. Baltimore, MD: Health Professions Press, 1995.

Ross, Austin, and Mary Richardson. *Ambulatory Health Care: Case Studies for the Health Services Executive*. Chicago: Health Administration Press, 1996.

Showalter, J. Stuart, and Bernard D. Reams. *The Law of Hospital and Health Care Administration*. Chicago: Health Administration Press, 1993.

II. Bibliographies of Cases

Foundation of the American College of Healthcare Executives. *Case Studies on Health Administration*. The Foundation, One North Franklin Street, Suite 1700, Chicago, IL 60606-3491.

Harvard Business School. *The Directory of Harvard Business School Cases*. Harvard Business School of Publishing, Customer Service Department, 60 Harvard Way, Boston, MA 02163-9907.

Kennedy School of Government. *The Directory of the Kennedy School of Government Cases*. Kennedy School, Harvard University, 79 John F. Kennedy Street, Cambridge, MA, 02138.

III. On Case Method

Christensen, C. Roland, with Abby Hansen. *Teaching and the Case Method*. Boston: Harvard Business School, 1987.

Christensen, C. Roland, et al. (eds.). *Education for Judgment: The Artistry of Discussion Leadership*. Boston: Harvard Business School, 1991.

Towl, Andrew R. *To Study Administration by Cases*. Boston, MA: Harvard University, Graduate School of Business Administration, 1969.

Index

Accountable, accountability, 6, 14, 23–31, 37–39, 77, 78, 79, 80, 91, 94, 102, 131, 151–189

Accountant, certified public accountant (CPA), accounting, accounting department, 13, 26, 27–31, 109–113, 118, 137

Access, 16, 45, 47, 91, 101, 102, 111, 112, 121, 141, 154

Accreditation, accrediting agencies, 66, 141, 155, 156, 163, 170

Adaptation, adaptive capability, 27–31, 102, 129–149, 154, 169–187, 188–189

Administration, administrator, 9–21, 23, 42–51, 55, 56, 57, 64, 78, 80, 84, 86, 99, 100, 123–124, 131, 149, 171, 178

Admissions, admitting department, 44, 48, 54, 108, 125, 142, 159, 166, 181

Ambulatory, 77, 125, 158, 167

Ambulatory care, 4, 10, 17, 24, 39, 75, 77, 84, 121, 126, 144

Ancillary services, 160

Appointments, patient, 10, 112–113, 147

Authority, 4, 27, 103, 176

Autonomy, 16, 27, 77, 78, 94, 107

Average length of stay (ALOS), 64, 121, 127. *See* Length of stay (LOS)

Benefit plan, 94

Billing(s), billing systems, 10, 11, 13, 15, 16, 20, 23, 26, 79, 108, 110, 114, 118, 148

Blue Cross, 99, 140, 182

Board of trustees, trustees, 42–43, 64, 66–67, 73, 83, 84, 85–86, 87, 90, 91, 92–93, 94, 95, 96, 100, 103, 104, 108, 109, 114, 125, 131, 133, 136, 137, 139, 140, 143, 153, 155, 156, 157, 169–187; governance, 66–67, 73, 92–93, 103, 139

Board of directors, 53, 59

Budget, budgeting, xviii, 28, 29, 30, 37, 102, 126, 176

Business school, xviii–xix, xxi, 174

Bylaws, 85, 86; medical staff, 101

Capitation, 71, 76, 107, 111, 112, 121

Case method, xi–xiv, xv–xxii

Census, hospital, 175

Chief executive officer (CEO), xviii, 9, 57, 81, 95, 125, 126, 132, 169–187

Chief operating officer (COO), 32, 53–54, 58, 66, 75–82, 91, 117–124, 127, 135, 157, 188

Collaboration, 90, 92, 141

About the Editors

Anthony R. Kovner, M.P.A., Ph.D., is Professor of Health Policy and Management at the Robert F. Wagner Graduate School of Public Service at New York University. He has served as Senior Program Consultant to the Robert Wood Johnson Foundation and the W. K. Kellogg Foundation. Dr. Kovner is a member of the Board of Trustees of Lutheran Medical Center in Brooklyn, New York. Before joining NYU, he was Chief Executive Officer of the Newcomb Hospital of Vineland, New Jersey, and Senior Health Consultant to the United Auto Workers Union in Detroit, Michigan. He is co-author, with Alan Channing, of *Really Trying: A Career Guide for the Health Services Manager*, Second Edition (1993) and *Really Managing: The Work of Effective CEOs in Large Health Organizations* (1988). He is co-author, with Duncan Neuhauser, of *Health Services Management: Readings and Commentary*, Sixth Edition.

Duncan Neuhauser, M.H.A., M.B.A., Ph.D., is Professor of Epidemiology and Biostatistics, with secondary professorships in Medicine, Family Medicine, and Organizational Behavior. He is co-director of the Health Systems Management Center, all at Case Western Reserve University, Cleveland, Ohio. His prior collaboration with Anthony R. Kovner resulted in *Health Services Management: Readings and Commentary*. His book *Coming of Age*, Second Edition, a sixty-year history of the American College of Health Care Executives, was published in 1994. For 15 years, he has been editor of *Medical Care*.